WHY DEBATE

TRANSFORMED BY ACADEMIC DISCOURSE

SHAWN F. BRISCOE
LEAD AUTHOR AND EDITOR

MY DEBATE RESOURCES

Paperback ISBN 0-9978684-0-6 (978-0-9978684-0-1)
eBook ISBN 0-9978684-1-4 (978-0-9978684-1-8)

My Debate Resources

Formatting by www.ebooklaunch.com

DEDICATION

Many thanks to my wonderful wife, Becky, who always encourages me to pursue my dreams, even when they seem outlandish, costly, and likely to give her a headache as I obsess over them. Thank you for being my best friend, partner, and confidant.

To Ben & Hannah - I love you more than words can say.

ACKNOWLEDGMENTS

Many thanks to the authors who contributed a piece of themselves to this project. Paul, thank you for helping me navigate the publishing process. Marshall & Ryan, thanks for telling me your stories. Ultimately, they were the inspiration for this project. Becky, thank you for all the encouragement along the way. Coaches & judges everywhere - thank you for your incredible support of students. You are literally the reason students reap the rewards detailed in this work.

Table of Contents

Introduction

This book stems from my firm belief that debate is one of the most powerful forces in modern society. Researchers, academics, think tanks, politicians, and members of committees engage one another in active discourse in an attempt to ascertain the source of problems present in our society. Then, they take part in an intellectual back-and-forth to determine the proper course of action.

Within our schools there is an extracurricular and co-curricular activity that pushes students to think about issues beyond their immediate surroundings. Perhaps, more importantly, this activity teaches students to think critically, to analyze information put before them, to consider potential outcomes, to think about the principles that ought to drive our actions, and to present their ideas in a coherent manner. While the activity is first and foremost an academic exercise, it is situated within a competitive framework that offers additional insights into how to handle oneself under pressure, how to work effectively with others, and so forth.

Despite its importance, this activity is often invisible to the larger student population whose members do not even know it exists. When they do, they often view the participants on those teams as geeks, nerds, dorks. Often, administrators, teachers, and students within the schools or around campus have a fundamental misunderstanding of what the activity actually is.

Nevertheless, academic or competitive debate should hold a unique place within our secondary and undergraduate education systems. Numerous studies have highlighted the benefits of debate, speech and debate, and forensics programs in our schools:

- Allen, M., Berkowitz, S., Hunt, S., & Louden, A. (1999). A meta-analysis of the impact of forensics and communication education on critical thinking [Electronic version]. *Communication Education*, 48(1), 18-30. http://eric.ed.gov/?id=EJ579165

- Anderson, S. & Mezuk, B. (2012). Participating in a policy debate program and academic achievement among at-risk adolescents in an urban public school district: 1997-2007. *Journal of Adolescence.* http://urbandebate.org/Portals/0/EmergingResearch/Journal%20of%20Adolescence%20(Mezuk%20et%20al).pdf

- Jones, D. (2004, September 30). Debating skills come in handy in business. *USA Today*, 3B. http://usatoday30.usatoday.com/educate/college/careers/news20.htm

- Mezuk, B., Bondarenko, I., Smith, S., & Tucker, E. "Impact of participating in a policy debate program on academic achievement: Evidence from the Chicago Urban Debate League." Educational Research and Reviews. (5 September 2011). http://urbandebate.org/Portals/0/EmergingResearch/Mezuk%20et%20al.pdf

What is missing is an examination of individuals reflecting on how debate shaped their lives and why. Two of my former teammates and I were talking a few years back, and they shared their thoughts with me about how debate impacted their professional lives. Those stories became the inspiration for and the basis of this book.

This anthology is not meant to push a single academic debate format, a unique style of debate, nor a specific level at which competition is most important. The authors of this book have a diverse background in styles, formats, and levels of experience.

Some of the authors competed exclusively in high school. Others did not begin competing until college. Some of them competed in both high school and college.

Some of the authors in this book competed exclusively on local debate circuits near their hometown. Others competed regionally or nationally. Still others competed internationally.

The authors of this book competed in high school policy, Lincoln Douglas, congress, and/or public forum. Other authors experienced the activity in college through the Cross Examination Debate Association, the National Debate Tournament, the National Parliamentary Debate Association, and/or British Parliamentary debate (as practiced at the World Universities Debating Championships).

Almost all of the authors in this book are directly connected to my life: former teammates, former students, and colleagues. Only a handful of them lack that personal connection with me. At first, my inclination was to seek out a diverse group of people who experienced the best of what the activity had to offer. Upon reflection, to do so could be seen as cherry picking the best examples who would serve my purpose in this work, but might not be representative of what the activity truly has to offer the vast majority of students who engage in it. Thus, it seemed the best way to demonstrate just how pervasive debate is in the lives of those who took part in it, was to draw from the experiences of those who experienced debate within my own, albeit very diverse, sphere of experience.

My goal in this work is to highlight just how impactful academic debate can be on the typical teenager or college student who walks into practice and asks, "Is this where the debate team meets?"

I hope you enjoy it as much as we did,

Shawn

Preface: Why I Fell in Love with Debate

By Shawn F. Briscoe

Educator & Forensics Coach

At one point, I was completely clueless about competitive, academic debate. I grew up in a rural town 100 miles south of Kansas City. Our high school had a regionally competitive speech and debate team. Our debate coach, Tim Gore, was one of the best coaches in Missouri, if not the country.

Despite excellent coaching, my partner and I did not really have any idea what we were doing when we went to our first tournament in Springfield, Missouri. For our first round, we were tasked with debating the negative side of that year's resolution, which called for increasing U.S. space exploration. There were really only two things that meant to us as we entered that first debate. 1) We could not read the affirmative case our coach helped us write. 2) We were supposed to disagree with the affirmative team by using things like Ts, Disads, and Ev. *Whatever those were supposed to mean.*

As the first affirmative speaker delivered his speech, we furiously tried to keep up with him and take notes. Then, we frantically tried to find arguments in our files that we thought might apply to what the affirmative speaker was saying. It did not go well. We all had trouble stringing together complete sentences, and the round was over almost as soon as it began. Our judge, a former debater, was very pleasant despite the anguish we must have put him through.

He offered to walk us through the round, explain how it was supposed to progress, and offer tips for the future. First step, he asked for our flows. The four of us competing looked blankly at each other and shrugged. The judge muffled a sigh and said "your notes from the round." At that point, the temperature in the room shot up to 98 degrees. Or, maybe I was just embarrassed. Our coach had shown us the best way to take notes, or *flow* the round, but my paper looked like random scribbling rather than an organized history of the round. Obviously, I was completely clueless.

Over the remainder of my freshman year, my knowledge and skills developed tremendously, mostly due to my coach. In addition to his teaching, I learned a lot from simply debating at more tournaments and observing some of the upperclassmen on the team. Most importantly, by the end of the year I had fallen in love with debate. Why?

The thrill of competition. Competing in a debate is a unique experience. It was similar to the experiences I felt when running track or playing soccer on my hometown's traveling soccer team. But, it was different. It was more personal. Prior to a debate round, and sometimes prior to a tournament, I could feel myself getting psyched up for the pending competition. As the round itself progressed, arguments unfolded in interesting ways, I saw openings in my opponents' strategy, I witnessed my own arguments being picked apart, and/or the tempo of the round quickened, I often received an adrenaline rush... odd as that may sound to someone who has never taken part in the activity.

The travel was a trip. No other competitive high school or college activity has a season almost as long as the school year. We routinely went all around the state as a team. We spent weekends together and built the bonds of friendship. Some college programs and high school teams traverse the entire nation over the course of the year. In fact, within the span of a single month during my sophomore year in college my teammates and I went from Eugene, OR, to Towson, MD, to Tuscaloosa, AL, to Long Beach, CA. Some college programs even travel the globe for competition. It is not uncommon to find debaters travelling to places like England, Turkey, Germany, Botswana, China, or Thailand.

It was exhausting. In a good way. High school tournaments typically started mid-afternoon on Friday and continued until late in the evening. Competition resumed dark and early Saturday morning and concluded well into the evening. (And those were the short tournaments.) Not only that, but debate can be quite mentally draining as well. After a day of living and breathing debate, the mind and the body are truly spent.

The competition is unique and diverse. Few other competitive activities are coed. Men and women compete in this activity as equals. There are no distinctions between small and large schools. 2A schools routinely compete against 4A schools. Division III schools regularly defeat Division I schools. State schools repeatedly crush Ivy League schools. And vice versa. The pool of competitors is large and varied, making competition more interesting and more cutthroat.

Speech can be a high. Carefully balancing speed with persuasion can be exhilarating. To quote the slogan of the 1996 Cross Examination Debate Association national championship tournament: "Speech is Life. Talk Hard."

These were the things that drew me to debate and led me to stick with the activity throughout high school. They led me to seek out the debate team at the United States Air Force Academy. They drove me to participate in the activity even though the Academy places more than just a few time constraints on its students. Those factors are not, however, what led me to volunteer with debate teams while I served on active duty in the Air Force nor what led me to leave a promising career as an officer so that I could serve students.

Debate is uniquely educational. Obviously, it is a speaking event, and trains students to speak clearly, even when it leads them to speak at seemingly incomprehensible rates. But, public speaking is not where the real benefit of the activity lies. Somewhere around my junior year in college, I realized that my time on the high school debate team did more to prepare me for college than anything else: extracurricular activities, leadership positions on competitive teams, honors and college preparation courses. They all paled in comparison. Debate taught me how to think critically, how to think quickly on my feet, how to organize my thoughts, how to research, how to write, and how to commit myself to self-improvement and team growth.

Debate also highlighted the interconnectedness between disciplines. Our education system is largely divided neatly into separate subjects that rarely overlap. In the real world, that simply isn't the case. For example, how can one understand the United States' energy policy without understanding the science behind fossil fuel consumption and the interplay of gases in the atmosphere or the interests and intentions of the various stakeholders in the policy process? Debate tears down the very fabric of this notion that things, people, and knowledge exist in a vacuum. Everything is connected.

As I transitioned to life in the Air Force, I missed debate. I missed the rigors of the activity, the camaraderie, and the thrill of competition. I also wanted others to benefit the way that I had. That led me to do two things: return to the world of running by training and entering road races and volunteer with local high school speech and debate teams. After a couple years serving as an officer in the Air Force, things were looking pretty good for me. I was excelling in my job and having a positive impact on the people and the mission.

As I reflected back, I came to another realization: my time on the USAFA debate team did more to prepare me for officership than any other program at the Academy. I do not say that to belittle the Air Force Academy. It is a remarkable institution, and I love it to this day. I say that to highlight how significant an impact debate had on me, by comparing it to one of the finest academic institutions in the world.

Debate not only had the benefits mentioned above, but I realized debate also helped me find the points of agreement between two seemingly opposed sides. It helped me track diverse thoughts in meetings and find ways to make sense of them and bring people together.

I remember sitting in meetings as a first lieutenant or captain (surrounded by lieutenant colonels, colonels, and generals) and being surprised by how heated conversations would get because people thought they were on opposite sides of an all-important issue. I got to the point that I would essentially start flowing the staff meeting in the manner a debate judge would, then pipe up and explain where the individuals in the room were actually in agreement. Often, that would lead to silence, and then the senior leadership would start coming together. Simply, debate taught me that issues are rarely as black and white as they seem, to think quickly and analytically during discussions, and to use disagreement as an opportunity for finding a bigger truth.

This ability to see the middle ground and empathize with another's perspective also helped me be a better leader for the people I worked with in the office. It helped me to understand others so that I could foster teamwork with those I supervised, my peers, and even my superiors. In short, debate was a training ground for developing the skills necessary for the workforce.

Ultimately, the activity played a significant role in shaping who I was as a person. Debate instilled a unique perspective that shaped my thoughts on leadership, community, and citizenship. In the end, debate transforms how people see the world. It opens doors, it invites dialogue, and it breeds understanding.

I am not alone in these beliefs. This book contains the stories of debaters who feel as I do: that debate is powerful. Debate is transformative.

Section I: The Nature of Debate

Debate is one of the most misunderstood concepts in contemporary society.

The masses and, indeed, mass media perceive debate as a hotly contested argument, in which the opposing sides bitterly fight one another through personal attacks, volume, and chest thumping.

Teenagers enter classroom debates with the goal of putting someone in his place. Debate is an opportunity to demonstrate superiority over another individual.

Administrators wonder why debate teams need professional coaches. You merely "tell the kids to stand up and talk." Why does that require a trained coach, let alone an educator?

Mainstream media features debate programs where participants hurl insults, talk over, and largely ignore the points made by those on the other side.

Political debate sees candidates relying on emotional appeals and preying on the pre-conceived opinions or prejudices of their base. At the extreme, it sees political elites fueling the flames of fear and hate to drown out reasoned discourse.

Lawmakers resort to ad hominem attacks and package legislation with nifty titles like No Child Left Behind or the USA PATRIOT Act in order to misdirect attention from debate over the merits of the legislation.

Even those who walk off the street to view students engaged in academic debate are assaulted with what they perceive to be highly technical language spouted off at dizzying speed. Lest you think I am referring only to policy debate on the high school's national circuit or collegiate level, this is true of nearly any debate format. It is true when someone enters a room where high school Lincoln Douglas debaters are throwing out terms like value-criterion and debating the merits of Kantian ethics versus utilitarian consequentialism. It is true in, the decidedly audience-friendly, British Parliamentary format practiced at the World Universities Debating Championships when competitors from various nations with unique accents and colloquialisms toss about terms like model, extension, positive matter, and the like.

But, what is debate really? The following essays capture the true nature of academic debate and the experiences of students who dare to join the debate team.

A Guiding Force of History

By Dr. Minh A. Luong

Business Analytics Researcher
and Retired Academic & Forensics Coach

Critical thinking and superior communication skills form the foundation for intellectual advancement and effective leadership. The ability to write and speak informatively and persuasively, regardless of academic discipline and professional field, will be at the forefront of the most important skills for global leaders in the twenty-first century. Why? Perhaps the biggest reason is the challenges that will continue to affect humanity - the environment, energy supplies, global health, and access to food and clean water, to name just a few - are growing larger in scope and magnitude; requiring debate and cooperation across national boundaries and cultures.

Successfully meeting these challenges requires the wisest decisions from leaders around the world who are well-informed by advisers who are themselves leading experts in their respective fields. From determining the best information upon which to base policy to how to most effectively implement those policies, debate-oriented discussion will be the primary method by which important decisions are made by the world's leading societies and international organizations.

What is debate? The purest form of debate is when assumptions are themselves subject to debate so the discussion is not needlessly limited by artificial limitations or ideology. This is especially true in the case of scientific research where certain assumptions are held before any hypotheses are made. In fact, the scientific revolution began when Nicolaus Copernicus, the Polish Renaissance astronomer, lawyer, doctor, economist, and Catholic cleric, set aside Roman Catholic ideology and with it, assumptions about the Earth being the center of the universe, and demonstrated that celestial bodies did not orbit the Earth; instead, it was the Sun. Copernicus's heliocentric model took four decades to develop after much discussion and debate with fellow scientists and religious clerics. Copernicus died the day he received an advance copy of his masterpiece, *De revolutionibus orbium coelestium (On the Revolutions of the Celestial Spheres)* but on that day, 24 May 1543, the scientific revolution was born.

The practice of using debate as a truth-seeking, justice-serving, and policy-making methodology is not new and, in fact, has been utilized by many of the world's most advanced civilizations.

Cyrus the Great, who launched what was to later become the Persian Empire, was the first ruler in history to successfully conquer and govern a vast, multi-state empire with multiple capitals. He allowed a certain amount of regional autonomy and promoted education and exchange of ideas and innovation throughout his empire. In fact, Cyrus encouraged vigorous debate among his ministers and counselors and often debated with his subordinates on the opposite side of his beliefs in order to seek out the best course of action. But once the debate was over and the decision was made, Cyrus expected all of his officers and governors to implement the policy. For Cyrus, one of his guiding philosophies was "diversity in counsel; unity in command." Through these vigorous debates, Cyrus became one of the world's most progressive rulers.

Debate was also a major component of civic and political life in the great Greek societies. Aristotle's model of the persuasive speaker in his leadership treatise, *Treatise on Rhetoric*, highlighted three necessary elements of effective persuasion and policymaking:

- Ethos: Demonstrating good ethics and earning credibility in the minds of the audience
- Pathos: Showing genuine conviction through passion and emotion
- Logos: Use of solid logic and reasoning in supporting arguments and policies

Aristotle argued further that proper use of rhetoric, or persuasive communication, benefits society as a whole. The Greek philosophers Socrates, Plato, and Aristotle became very concerned that rhetoric was being used by unethical speakers and leaders, the Sophists, to control fellow citizens by manipulating their emotions and omitting key information. Aristotle's answer to the Sophists, built on top of ideas originated by Socrates and Plato, was to encourage enlightenment by bundling three different elements of philosophy:

- Logic: Scientific reasoning to find truth and clarity in knowledge
- Dialectic: Philosophical discussion to find truth and clarity in knowledge
- Rhetoric: Practical discussion to persuade listeners on a course of action or policy

In this manner, by pursing facts (logic), values (dialectic), and policies (rhetoric) in a rigorous, systematic manner, an educated public would not be subject to manipulation by unethical sophists and corrupt politicians.

The Qin Dynasty of China embraced debate as a means of academic and leadership training, as well. The Qin emperor adopted the legalistic approach to governance, promoted schools that trained young leaders in debate, and encouraged vigorous discussion to determine the best governance policies. While the rule of the Qin emperor was brief-only 15 years-China was reunited as one and the Qin pursued a wide range of policies that advanced trade and transportation. The Qin standardized the Chinese language, writing, and currency as well as weights and measurements. In the 21st Century, the Communist Party of the People's Republic of China (PRC) has implemented academic debate throughout its leadership training in high schools and colleges in the hopes of empowering future generations to debate and confront future problems, as well as develop the skills they need to engage Western leaders in business and government.

Debate and the vigorous exchange of information has been the historical hallmark of advanced societies. Their innovations in scientific inquiry, technological advancement, engineering, trade and commerce, and governance could not have been realized without an environment in which robust, vigorous debate was not only tolerated, but encouraged at all levels. No one culture or governance system has a monopoly on using debate, but a common trait these advanced societies possessed was that they used debate as a means for societal progress and stability. In more recent times, most members of the U.S. Congress were debaters in high school and/or college.

Preparing the leaders of tomorrow has become increasingly complex due to rapid changes in technology, demographics, migration, communications, commerce, and interaction with other countries and cultures in an interconnected world. Just a few generations ago, it was sufficient to focus on a single vocation and be knowledgeable about the affairs of your immediate surroundings-the city or village where you lived, for example. Two generations ago, it was sufficient to have a general education in several disciplines and be knowledgeable about your province. But today's high school and college students need a far more comprehensive education in order to compete, thrive, and lead in the global economy.

The foundation of education consists of a broad knowledge base of different subjects ranging from mathematics and science to history and geography. Nearly every nation has an educational system that supports student learning in this manner. The key difference in the twenty-first century, however, is that rote learning (memorization and recitation) and amassing facts and equations without understanding context and application are insufficient for personal, professional, and societal advancement since information itself cannot help students master complex concepts at an advanced level. This is especially true in the United States where high-stakes testing has been emphasized over synthesis, creativity, and application. Academic debate is one of the very few intellectual pursuits that transcends these obstacles.

In order to promote deeper learning and understanding as well as to promote applied thought to challenging problems, more nations are incorporating critical thinking and debate into their school curricula as a means to help students (and later professionals) analyze and select the best data, theories, methodologies, and policies. This new approach promotes understanding of knowledge within a context and application of knowledge to both theoretical and empirical problem solving.

Here are just some of the benefits of participating in debate:

- *You may become a more critical thinker.* Debate teaches you to evaluate and select the best information and arguments while avoiding bias and logical fallacies. Using sound logic and reasoning not only helps you be a better student but also more effective in discussions at home and in your professional career.

- *You may become more open-minded.* Debate mandates that you prepare for as many arguments as possible on both sides of the topic. By conducting comprehensive research on many facets of the topic, you gain exposure to a wide range of thought. By thinking carefully about the best research on the topic, you may find your existing opinions confirmed or that you need to change your opinion in light of better information.

- *You may become more creative.* Many people who do not participate in the activity think that debate is merely the recitation of facts. In actuality, debate not only requires the collection and analysis of information but a large measure of creativity in how arguments are constructed and supported. Debate promotes the type of creative thinking that sparks innovative approaches to complex problems and issues.

- *You will interact with people who have different ideas and perspectives.* Smart people who think that their way is the only way have great difficulty interacting with people who have ideas different from their own. Their ability to contribute to an organization or society is significantly reduced due to their lack of ability to engage in debate and incorporate new ideas and thinking into their own. Participation in debate may give you the ability to connect with other people who have different ideas and perspectives and through the critical thinking process, develop ideas that are more advanced than what you held previously.

- *You may learn effective teamwork skills.* Because debate is a group activity that is information and solutions-focused, you may be more comfortable working in a team environment. The benefits of team discussion and problem solving are well-documented and spirited debate in groups promotes more comprehensive and practical solutions than those that are developed by a single person or a group of like-minded individuals.

- *You may learn the value of meeting stakeholder needs and compromise.* Every organization and nation has different stakeholders and needs. Debate encourages discussion and solutions that address the needs of the various stakeholders, not just one. In order to progress forward, some compromise may be necessary to obtain the support of the stakeholders. Discussion through debate promotes an examination of the needs of all stakeholders and, if necessary, what compromises are needed for the best solution for all.

- *Excellent preparation for college-level work.* The world's top universities recognize that many of the best students have previous experience in debating and that those students are ready to learn and apply advanced concepts because they already are competent and confident in their critical thinking and research skills and can demonstrate their knowledge by strong writing and public speaking skills. That is why talented high school students who excel in debating win admission to the world's leading universities at a significantly higher rate than students who did not participate in debate.[1]

Furthermore, your country and the global community benefit from leaders who engage in vigorous debates:

- *Innovation and advancement of science and technology.* Debate among scientists and policymakers is essential to advance the frontiers of science and technology to address global challenges. As global problems become more pressing and require urgent action, the scientific

---

[1] This conclusion is as true after 2015 as it was when I first wrote on the subject at the beginning of the Millennium. In my Rostrum, November 2000 essay, "Forensics and College Admissions," I presented data from a Wall Street Journal study on selective college admissions rates that found a significant advantage for applicants with public speaking and debating experience. After countless discussions and interviews with college admissions officers, directors, and deans, this advantage has grown even more pronounced since the publication of the essay over 15 years ago. Many admission officers complain that "grade inflation is rampant," "the pervasiveness of applicants who have gone through standardized test preparation renders SAT and ACT scores useless," and personal statements and letters of recommendation "all sound the same." The key differentiator is demonstrated success in the very skill that has determined success in the classroom and beyond: The ability to logically construct sound arguments and effectively persuade others. Writing effectiveness is important but in this video-oriented, media-intensive generation, effective public speaking and debate skills are absolutely vital. Success in academic debate has, over time, proven to be one of the best indicators of success, both in college and career.

community does not have the luxury of time. Vigorous debate will help the scientific community and policymakers select the most promising approaches that will yield the best results. In a time of global resource scarcity, policymakers will find it impossible to fund all possible proposals. Debating the merits of each proposal will help policymakers to select which proposals deserve support.

- *Superior governance and leadership.* Debate encourages discussion of issues based on objective data and clearly defined criteria for selected solutions. Because issues are decided based on the merits of the proposals supported by unbiased information, leaders are in an advantageous position to select the best policies for the good of the people.

- *Maintaining social stability and development.* Advanced societies eschew violence as a means for resolving disputes and conflicts. As a non-violent avenue for conflict resolution, debate is the preferred method of identifying and resolving differences of opinions and interests as well as establishing solutions acceptable to relevant stakeholders.

Today's debaters are the next generation of national and global leaders and the analytical tools and communication skills they learn through debate will make them better students and leaders. They join a global fraternity of debaters who are committed to helping their communities, countries, and the world in an increasingly challenging era.

Dr. Minh A. Luong was the U.S. National Collegiate Champion and Top Speaker in Lincoln-Douglas Debate and later served as director of public speaking and debate at the University of California at Berkeley. He also served as the founding curriculum director of the high school Lincoln-Douglas debate institutes at Stanford University, the University of California at Berkeley, and the National Debate Forum (NDF) [various campuses]. A life member of the National Forensic League, Dr. Luong authored and edited numerous articles on argumentation and debate, helped run several of the largest debate tournaments in the U.S. for over 20 years, and edited the NFL Lincoln-Douglas debate topic tutorials sponsored by PlanetDebate and Harvard Debate from 2003 to 2012. He taught at Brown University in international affairs, political science, and public policy, and continues to teach online leadership courses through Brown's School of Professional Studies (SPS). Dr. Luong has served every year since 2008 as a consultant to the United Nations Institute for Training and Research (UNITAR) at United Nations headquarters in New York City where he trains ambassadors and diplomats in public speaking, multilateral negotiations, cross-cultural communication, and UN Security Council Statement Writing and Presentations. He recently retired from his positions as director of the Ivy Scholars Program, associate director of the Brady-Johnson Program in Grand Strategy, assistant director of International Security Studies, and faculty advisor of the world championship Yale Debate Team, all at Yale University, after many years of service. He now works for a privately held German global research conglomerate that supports over 500 household brand names and icons. He uses his debate skills every day. Dr. Luong can be reached at his public service organization, National Debate Education Project at: NDEP@hotmail.com

Debate Is

By Shawn F. Briscoe

Educator & Forensics Coach

Civil discourse is critical to a democratic society. It is essential for creating an informed citizenry, combatting injustice, and crafting beneficial policy. Unfortunately, what passes for debate in contemporary society leaves much to be desired. Too many venues claiming to advance debate on any given controversial topic devolve into assertions vocalized loudly, unsubstantiated claims, and ad hominem attacks against supporters of the other side. All too often, students wishing to join competitive debate teams or enroll in debate courses have been convinced these tendencies define debate. Nothing could be further from the truth. True academic debate goes much deeper than those examples prevalent in our society.

Debate is many things. Academic debate is full of seemingly contradictory, yet synergistic, principles. Debate is both disagreement and agreement. Debate is competitive, yet social. Debate is complex, but simple. Despite being rooted in argumentation, debate is not about arguments. Debate and the advancement of arguments are not reliant on statements of belief. They are not questions. They are not assertions. They are not fights. They are, however, logically connected ideas that prove a point. They require agreement from both sides of the issue as much as they require disagreement. Truly, debate is many things.

Debate is structured. For example, policy debate abounds with structures that drive the debate and the learning process. Each year, the National Federation of High Schools and the Cross Examination Debate Association select the annual debate topic for high schools and colleges around the country. That topic establishes parameters for debates. The organizations governing debate activities set the number of speeches and speaker orders for the participants. Each student is granted two speeches with specified time limits to advance his or her positions. Students may not interrupt one another while their opponent is speaking. Even cross-examination periods dictate that one person asks questions while the other may only answer them. Sides are selected for the students, meaning they are told minutes before the debate begins whether they will argue in favor of or against the resolution or topic. A myriad of norms and conventions encourage and discourage certain behaviors in the debate round.

Nevertheless, **debate is creative.** The very structures of the activity and norms used in judging encourage debaters to explore argumentation. They may experiment with new types of arguments and strategies. They may inject themselves into the debate as they become co-creators of knowledge with their opponents. The best debaters extend themselves beyond the quoted evidence by providing their own unique analysis of the evidence, issues, and strategies used by themselves and their opponents. Debate is not static. It grows; it changes; it becomes something more with each generation of debaters.

Debate is disagreement. At the core of every debate are two debate teams engaged in a clash of ideas. The debate topic serves to divide ground on an issue of significance, tasking each team to advance arguments in favor of or in opposition to the given resolution. For every point offered, three or four responses may be levied. Both sides present arguments to construct their cases, while also attempting to deconstruct those offered by the other side.

Nevertheless, **debate is agreement.** Debate cannot progress unless both sides agree on some fundamental points. They must agree on the overarching topic. They must agree to engage one another on the points of significance offered by one another. They learn that often, the key to persuasion requires the individual to acknowledge the legitimacy of the other side. Finding the point at which both sides agree is crucial to generating empathy and reaching agreement on the bigger issues.

Debate is complex. The ideas and concepts discussed on any given debate topic have their place in graduate level studies and texts. Observers from the community are overwhelmed by the complexity of thought and critical thinking displayed by participants. The jargon rolling off the tongues of competitors sounds foreign to the uninitiated. From personal experience, I can tell you that the degree of analysis and depth of exploration of ideas rivaled or surpassed that of any course I took in high school, college, or graduate school.

Nevertheless, **debate is simple.** Two teams assigned to defend opposite sides of the resolution. Their only task: be more persuasive than their opponents and convince the judge to reward them with a ballot. The jargon, which may be intimidating to the novice, actually references simple tools and concepts for understanding complicated ideas. They can be used to understand an argumentative stance, break down a complex idea, develop a position, or engage someone in constructive discourse whether it takes place in a debate round, a science class, a staff meeting, or on the pages of a research paper. Although many of the ideas in a debate round may seem advanced and difficult to understand, the structures of debate create a simple framework for understanding.

Debate is competitive. The thrill of competition drives many students to participate, research, and learn. Odd as it may sound, the adrenaline rush of a debater can be every bit as powerful as that of an athlete. Debaters engage one another in mental sparring matches, racking up wins and losses, earning speaker awards and championships. Universities seeking publicity for their academic prowess offer debate scholarships just as they offer them for football and basketball. This focus on competition is the fuel for many debaters.

Nevertheless, **debate is social.** Debate squads become close-knit teams helping one another and enjoying the success of their peers. Teams regularly become second families for many participants. Not only that, but the debate circuit tends to be rather communal. Unlike sports teams where competitors usually only see each other across the line of scrimmage or on opposite sides of a field, debaters necessarily interact with one another before, during, and after rounds. They form friendships with competitors from other squads. They cheer the success of students from rival schools and feel for them when they are handed a tough loss. They often offer advice to one another, making suggestions for improving an argument or providing an opponent a critical piece of evidence that was lacking. Even coaches from opposing teams offer high quality feedback to students from other teams.

Debate is independent. Every participant must stand on his or her own. She must be prepared to hold the floor for an eight minute constructive speech and a five minute rebuttal. Ultimately, she must use her own analysis to present a sound case and engage critically with her opponents.

Nevertheless, **debate is teamwork.** Most debate formats incorporate two-person teams. Debaters succeed and fail alongside a partner. They work together before the tournament to ensure they are prepared. They must cooperate in round to ensure a cohesive strategy. They must trust one another to do their jobs. Failure to work together, cooperate, or trust one another ultimately undermines their ability to succeed or reach their maximum potential. In addition, debate squads prepare together. The best teams look out for one another. As the saying goes, a rising tide floats all boats. As the team gets better, so do all its debaters. Many circuits even take this to the next level, working across team lines for the betterment of all.

Debate is homogenous. The activity is filled with many like-minded individuals. Debaters are intellectual. They like to grapple with big ideas. They love to use their own analysis and rhetoric to make them accessible to the judge.

Nevertheless, **debate is uniquely integrated.** Unlike most competitive activities, there are no artificial divisions between groups of people. Small schools compete with large schools. Rich school districts compete with poor school districts. Private schools compete with public schools. Urban schools compete with rural schools. Women compete with men.

Debate is local. Every team has a circuit with which it becomes intimately familiar. The lay judge circuits of Missouri share common judges and argumentative strategies. The competitors on that circuit know one another by sight and name. They develop a love-hate relationship with some of them. Just across the border in Kansas is another relatively insulated circuit with more progressive strategies and judges. Even the national circuit is, in a sense, local. The competitors travelling to events that promise legs for qualifying to the Tournament of Champions know each other very well, have a relatively homogeneous judging pool, and are at the forefront of new debate theory and practices. The competitors, judges, norms, conventions, and strategies used on a school's primary circuit seem as familiar to the participants as their own neighborhood.

Nevertheless, **debate is national and global.** Debate topics typically deal with issues of national or global significance. In addition, most teams have some opportunity to venture out of their neighborhood whether it be to attend a large invitational tournament in the area, crossing the border for exposure to debaters and judges in another state, or to compete at one of the national championship tournaments hosted by the National Speech & Debate Association, the National Catholic Forensic League, the National Debate Coaches Association, or the National Association for Urban Debate Leagues. There are even opportunities for debaters to interact with students from other nations through the high school World Schools Debate format or the collegiate British Parliamentary debate format practiced at the World Universities Debating Championship and invitational tournaments across the globe.

Debate is overwhelming. Every debater experiences the lows of feeling unprepared, outmatched, and uninformed. Often, the real educational experience in debate stems from coming to the realization that we do not know everything, by highlighting the things unknown to us. I recall my very first debate round. I seemingly forgot everything my coach taught me. I could barely string together a complete sentence. I was not alone. My partner and my opponents were equally as lost. A debate round that should have spanned an hour and a half took approximately twenty minutes. I was embarrassed. I questioned my intellect. I doubted whether this activity had a place for me.

Nevertheless, **debate is inspiring.** Just four tournaments later, I found myself in the championship round of another novice tournament. As I began my final speech, I made eye contact with Chad Mathis, one of the varsity debaters on my squad. I do not recall if I actually said anything intelligent, but Chad lightly grabbed his chin and nodded. At that moment, I felt powerful. I felt like I had something important to say and everyone else would see something extraordinary. This cycle of confusion and confidence, powerlessness and authority occurs many times throughout a debater's career. Not only does the cycle occur from year to year, but often from tournament to tournament, and occasionally during the span of a single debate round.

Debate is defensive. As an activity, debaters are tasked to defend one of side of the topic. As such, they mount a formidable defense of it. A snapshot of the activity sees two opposing sides locked in verbal combat.

However, **debate is transformative.** The very nature of switch-sides debate means that students are required to see and understand both sides of the topic. To truly engage their opponents, they must be able to see the opposition's point of view. Furthermore, they begin to understand the world is not black and white. There are no absolutes. They begin to see shades of gray. They begin to see points of mutual agreement when having a disagreement with friends or observing a discussion at a meeting. They start to see similarities between themselves and those whom they thought to be different. Debate helps us understand the world more completely and to see shared purpose with others.

Debate is all these things and many more.

Lasting Impressions

By Kari Jahnsen

Student at the Massachusetts Institute of Technology (MIT)

The spare room in my parents' house serves as an occasional guest room and a full-time graveyard for miscellaneous junk. Old Halloween costumes clog the tiny closet, neatly stacked boxes of well-loved but forgotten books line the perimeter, and a medium-sized bookshelf in the furthest corner holds the finest items of this resting place for memories. Here lies my mother's high school yearbook, books written in my father's first tongue, and a small shrine of sorts to my years as a juvenile. The obligatory elementary school projects clutter the lower shelves, binders of certificates from my volunteer work and academic career fill the middle shelves, elevated physically and metaphorically.

At the absolute top of this tower of collected memories sits a neat stack of five plastic cases. Inside these cases are a few of the accomplishments that I consider to be my greatest. Inside each of these cases rests a small bronze medallion attached to a ribbon. Four of these state championship ribbons are blue and the final is white. These are the physical embodiments of the pinnacle of my debate success; one would expect them to be displayed proudly, or at least kept somewhere more prominent than in a lonely room of lonelier objects. Yet, this is their home; ribbons fading with age and sun damage, and dust slowly gathering in spite of my mother's meticulous and impressive dedication to dust eradication.

I am still incredibly honored and proud to hold those awards. Yet, with each passing day that separates me from my time as a debater, those silly little medals mean less and less. I was fortunate to find success in debate; I was truly blessed to find happiness over the course of three years.

While I think everyone looks back on their middle school self and cringes a bit, when I recall my younger self I positively squirm with discomfort. Not only did I possess an unusual knack for social awkwardness, I was also afflicted with crippling introversion and shyness. I spoke in class, perpetually a more annoying and pedantic version of Hermione Granger, but when it came to connecting with my peers, I found myself unable to summon a single syllable. I had a few friends, but in all fairness, they were more friends of situational convenience than any depth, and only one lasted through my high school years. To cut it brief, my mother had to lecture me to go have fun and quit studying, which is the extreme opposite of the typical parental lecture.

After my freshman year of high school, my mother suggested the debate team. Of course, I was skeptical at first, especially of my teammates. They all seemed like the effervescent extroverts who would never befriend a dork like me. Yet, within a month, I felt myself drawn into their ranks and into what would become my second family.

For the first time, I found a community, a niche, where I felt like I belonged. Brilliant, talented people surrounded me from every angle, but they never made me feel like I was less than them, even as a novice. Everyone I had the privilege to meet demonstrated humility, kindness, and compassion at levels I have not found in any other group of people. I think that is one of the many things I love most about the debate community-a sense of collective caring. In the greater realm of high school, we contended with the label of super nerds, a trait I previously used as a shield to protect me from letting anyone in. On the team, everyone was a nerd, albeit in their own wonderfully unique ways. Since everyone existed on the same social plane with a known common interest, it was all too easy for them to begin to coax me out of my shell. As a result, I started, to my mother's eternal delight, to make friends.

This was kind of monumental, to say the least. I am still slightly boggled by why all these incredible, hilarious, and loving people would choose to associate themselves with a sarcastic and goofy individual like me. I feel unworthy of their friendship sometimes, not because I think I don't deserve it, but because I don't see how anyone could. That's how spectacular my friends are.

So when I look back on my debate career, I certainly remember winning each of the medallions, but I remember my teammates' place in these moments more clearly. I remember nearly squeezing my novice partner's hand off waiting for our third place award, and her reassuringly squeezing mine back. Walking off of the stage after my first victory, and into the waiting hug of one of my mentors, Nicole, I was in shock. I remember her whispering to me how proud of me she was, and I remember how that was what demolished me into a teary mess. It wasn't the victory, but the connection with my peers.

I remember the cheers of my team in the audience as I and my three compatriots in policy debate embraced on the stage after closing out the final round as co-state champions. I remember nervously shifting next to my dear policy partner Jack as we awaited the results of international extemporaneous speaking, and how when it came down to us, he almost crushed me in a hug, always supportive of me. I remember actually crying on stage when we closed out policy for a second time, with the boys smothering me in that victorious group embrace for what would be the last time.

I can recall each of these moments vividly. The crinkling of my blazer, the feeling of tears fresh on my cheeks, the dull roar of the rest of my teammates—my family—all rooting for me. Yet, these aren't even the fondest memories I have from debate. As clichéd as it sounds, the little moments matter more to me now that I can look back with the pleasant sepia-colored lens of nostalgia.

I remember returning to my seat after a 2AR and always finding a sticky note from Jack stuck to my laptop, ranging from the incredibly sassy to the wrenchingly heartfelt. I still have a collection of my favorites in my laptop bag, including the one from our last round together that reduced me to a sniffling mess, in the unique way only debate-related things can.

I remember sitting in an IHOP at 2 a.m. at my first national circuit tournament, downing a nutritious dinner of waffles drenched in syrup. Skyler said something so hilarious, in the way that all things said past midnight are, that I laughed so hard I started snorting. Of course, my loving teammates strove to repeat this special phenomenon at every opportunity. Jack currently holds the record at a seemingly unassailable fifty consecutive snorts.

I remember the constant ridiculousness and hilarity of team bus rides to tournaments. Quin attacking Dakota with plastic dinosaurs comes to mind, as does our tradition of holding sing-alongs. And how could I forget the many times I had to veto Dakota's Meghan Trainor collection? Executive vetoes well used in the opinion of all but Dakota.

I remember the antics of debate rounds against my team-mates. Our rounds were often competitive and taxing, but were always friendly. However, I much preferred casually discussing the zombie apocalypse with Zach during cross-examination my novice year to debating mass transit. I remember illustrating the Aliens Counterplan with Shruti, who at the time I hardly knew, but who is now one of my closest friends.

I remember all of the little miscellaneous moments I shared with my teammates that defy categorization. I remember all the times Terek expanded my musical horizons, and the one time I shocked him with my lyrical mastery of Soulja Boy. I remember the hilarity of Skyler and Quin crashing a dance at Dimond when our bus was late. I remember Tyanna crafting my war braids on Saturday mornings while we discussed her Lincoln-Douglas debate cases. I remember the flawless color coordination Jack and I sported at every tournament, especially on Murica Saturdays. I remember chasing after Terek and Skyler with an enraged Shruti after they absconded with our tub at Arizona State University. I remember Garrett regaling me with accurate interpretations of pantomimes that made me laugh so hard, I skipped snorting to go straight to crying with laughter. I remember sharing the most perfect high-five of my life with Jack at my final regular season tournament.

I remember bonding with members of the debate community as well. I remember a particularly cutthroat competitor offering to share evidence after one of the hardest rounds I ever endured on the national circuit. I remember all of the opponents I debated at home, and how we became friends outside of the rounds where we were staunch opponents. I remember breaking the "no talking in draw" rule with Lilian. I remember bribing Sam, with a pound of Skittles, to be my Northern Lights British Parliamentary debate partner. I remember the bittersweet goodbyes with everyone at the conclusion of my final season.

All of us coasted through the highs and the lows of competition together; I cried on my fair share of shoulders and offered up my own for them as well. Debate is an emotional rollercoaster where sometimes the only seatbelts holding you in place are your friends. I was lucky to have great ones.

When I was competing, I cared about winning. I cared about it a lot. I felt this massive, consuming need to prove myself, and so I prioritized doing many events and racking up awards. I realize now how utterly naïve and stupid I was. Sure, the awards looked good on a resume, certificates offer tangible proof of success, and medals shine with the seductive promise of accomplishment, but those things, while physical, are immaterial. This activity made me grow into myself, find my voice, and offered me a sense of belonging. I can't imagine my life without debate and the people I met through it. I can imagine my life without the small pile of medals, spiffy plaques, and thick binder of certificates. That life would be just as happy as the one I am living now. That life would still see me as a more confident, outgoing, and compassionate individual. That life would still have the amazing, fulfilling friendships and external family I love. That life would still encompass the most important aspects of my time as a debater.

A few physical steps from the spare room and my medals are my own domain. However, the emotional divide between the objects in that room and in this room is enormous. I like to keep a small collection of items on my nightstand. Of course, some are mundane, like a lamp and clock radio. The other items, however, are things I like to keep close to me because they are physical reminders of my happiest times. Sitting prominently and proudly next to the lamp is a small, framed picture. The picture is a relative newcomer, taken just before my graduation from high school. It features the seniors of my team, jubilant and joyful, clustered together in our debate sweatshirts. These are some of the people I love most in the world. These people are the most meaningful part of my debate experience. While my medals collect dust, my appreciation for my friends will remain untarnished. My sincere gratitude to the debate community for cultivating my growth as a young adult and for teaching me that what really matters in life will remain equally unblemished.

Kari Jahnsen is currently an undergraduate at MIT. She intends to pursue a degree in Economics. Kari debated for three years in high school, where she was honored to debate both at the state and national levels. She finished her debate career as an Academic All American and as a Quintuple Ruby holder (both in the National Speech & Debate Association). Even though she has officially retired from the policy debate life, Kari can still be found debating with her ex-Nat Circuit roommate (and anyone else who will listen) about everything from Star Wars to Neoliberalism Kritiks.

Section II: A Foundation for Growth

I have long maintained that debate is about two fundamental notions: community and growth. My goals for students never include competitive success. I do not evaluate my effectiveness as a coach on wins and losses or championships won. Rather, my goals for students are two-fold: *Have fun. And, learn something.*

The debate team (or forensics team or speech and debate team) brings students together in a social, academic, and competitive environment.

Students work together.

Students play together.

Competitions bring people from diverse backgrounds together in a social and competitive setting.

Competitors and coaches from opposing teams offer advice and support to one another.

Participation in the activity fosters growth. Students learn to exhibit grace under pressure: in success and failure. Students learn who they are and forge personal identities. They learn how to navigate complex ideas. They gain experience presenting their ideas to others. They learn to identify points of common interest. The list goes on.

The essays in this section explore the benefits of academic debate while the student is actively participating in it, but also how it prepares them academically for the challenges ahead.

Forensics:
Enhancing Civic Literacy & Democracy

By Shawn F. Briscoe

Educator & Forensics Coach

This chapter was originally published in 2009 as an article for Principal Leadership. *In addition to exploring the academic benefits of debate, it also discusses the other major pillars of competitive forensics: speech and interpretation of literature. Although I broke the article into three separate pillars, I believe that all of the benefits of speech and interpretation of literature are also present - to a lesser degree - in academic debate.*[2]

Forensics is, at its core, a discipline rooted in cross-curriculum study. Those engaged in the activity analyze, dissect, and interpret various forms of literature from multiple disciplines as they work against and *with* their competitors to advance their knowledge of content and to develop their communication skills. It is one way to address the problem that

> engaged citizens do not materialize out of thin air. They do not naturally grasp such knotty principles as tolerance, impartial justice, the separation of church and state, the needs for limits on majority power, or the difference between liberty and license. (Parker, 2006, p. 49)

---

[2] Briscoe, Shawn F. "Forensics: Enhancing Civic Literacy and Democracy," Principal Leadership. (May 2009): 44-49. Copyright (2009) National Association of Secondary School Principals. www.nassp.org. Reprinted with permission.

Put another way, simply presenting ideas to students and having them recite information from memory does little to instill understanding. Instead, students must explore the concepts to see how they developed, the circumstances from which they sprang, and how they affect people in the real world. To gain perspective on the issues, students must also be exposed to multiple viewpoints and surrounded by people from different backgrounds.

Regrettably, the educational system is a bureaucracy that inherently imposes rigid structures on teachers and students alike. As a result, the reality of "most formal education in the United States... is that it] emphasized dichotomous thinking" (Martin & Nakayama, 2004, p. 63). Too often, students learn to think in rigid—and often false—dichotomies, such as black and white, good and evil, male and female, hot and cold, and right and wrong. This thought process is even reflected in the overt curriculum as content is isolated into distinct subjects that rarely overlap in the classroom.

Thinking in this way can be both misleading and dangerous. Subjects are not unrelated fields; they almost always overlap and build on one another. Students who think in absolutes or stereotypes are hindered in their ability to truly grasp an idea or know and respect those who appear to be different from them. Rather than thinking in rigid absolutes, students should be encouraged to embrace the truth within multiple views, discovering how they combine and work together to elicit a clearer perception of reality.

Likewise, teachers should help students develop the tools they will use to develop well-thought out arguments that support their views. If students receive the freedom to think issues through, they are much more likely to truly grasp the underlying theories and implications. Further, they will be empowered to develop their own novel solutions to societal problems. Meanwhile, teachers are responsible for helping students build frameworks for understanding those issues. One way to achieve those aims in a socially responsible manner is to frame them within the bounds of a civic education.

Rhetorical Competence and Literacy

Cocurricular forensics programs consist of three types of competitive events—interpretative, competitive, and dialectical—all of which have their own unique and often overlapping benefits. The first is commonly referred to as *interpretation of literature*. Competitors in these events recreate the characters in a published story, making them seem living and real to the audience. Ultimately, the audience should feel as though they are watching the story unfold in real life. Because the event is devoid of costumes and props, students must employ a number of rhetorical devices and purposeful body language to effectively get their point across to the audience. Further, competitors often take on the persona of multiple characters within a single performance, so the development of these communications skills becomes even more pronounced. Aside from public speaking skills, there are other, more direct, connections to the standard curriculum.

First, interpretative competitors immerse themselves in literature. That is, one aspect of interpretation that makes it unique is that each student is responsible for choosing his or her piece. Because interpretative competitors may select any published literature, they pour over countless titles, including novels, short stories, plays, graphic novels, and poems. A typical semester in forensics might expose students to more literature—in terms of both quantity and variety—than a typical English class (McCrady, 2004). This increases students' literacy skills as they immerse themselves in the literature and also enhances the students' cultural literacy as they become increasingly familiar with classical and contemporary writings.

Second, interpretation extends beyond mere performance. Students are not judged solely on their ability to act or perform. In fact, one of the key elements looked for by most judges is the literary merit and social significance of the chosen piece. In other words, a student performing humorous interpretation may experience some success if the piece is funny and the delivery captures that humor, but the student is considerably more likely to receive high marks if he or she effectively demonstrates what the piece has to say about the importance of interpersonal relationships, the marginalization of teens in contemporary society, or the effects of extreme polarization in the United States. This typically takes place on two levels: through the performance itself and in an introduction to the piece during which the student explains why he or she chose a particular piece of literature and what it means to him or her.

Finally, as the name of the event implies, a key element of this activity is that the students' performance is dictated by his or her interpretation of the literature. Rather than mimicking the performance of famous actors or relying solely on the author's original meaning, students are encouraged to interpret the words on the basis of their own academic, cultural, and life experiences. This is not to say that prior performances or the author's intent are ignored. The literature could not truly be interpreted by the student without taking those factors into account.

During interpretative events, students critically analyze literature on multiple levels, taking into account the author's meaning; the historical context of the selection; the evolving meaning of the literature through generations of revisiting it in alternative media forms; the context of the literature in contemporary society; and the student's own unique, thoughtful, and personal insights on the material.

Critical Thought

Like interpretation, competitive speech offers a number of educational benefits through two broad types of speech events: platform and extemporaneous speaking. Platform speaking events require students to conduct extensive research on a controversial issue of their choice and generally attempt to persuade the audience in some way. Extemporaneous speaking events, on the other hand, require students to be familiar with a wide range of issues significant to the United States or the international community. Here, students are given a very specific question on a current event and receive 30 minutes to prepare and organize a 7-minute speech.

The most obvious educational benefit of competitive speech is the development of public speaking and writing skills. First and foremost, the structure of a well-thought out speech becomes ingrained in students' thought process as they organize countless speeches throughout the season: attention getting device, clear thesis statement, preview, three main points, summary, and transition out of the speech. While preparing, they experiment with a number of organizational patterns, learning through personal experience how organizational structure influences the audiences' perception and understanding. Further, they learn how to use words and rhetorical devices to persuade and inform their audience effectively. Again, over the course of a forensics season, they have more opportunities to perfect their skills than a course in a public speaking could ever hope to afford.

Citizens in a democratic society are often called upon to persuade others of the best course of action, whether as political leaders, citizens engaged in discussions with peers in informal settings, or in a typical business setting. One forensics educator asserted that "perhaps even more important for the average person—who admittedly may never stand up to address large numbers of people—is the ability to recognize what is being done when other people stand up to do so" (Crawford, 2003, p. 2). By learning how to employ words in an effective and ethical manner, students are inoculated against misleading tactics that public speakers use in other situations.

Speech competitors also gain knowledge about a plethora of controversial topics. In platform events, such as original oratory, students are encouraged to select persuasive topics that alert the audience to a potential danger or strengthen devotion to a cause. Recent topics addressed by students at national competitive events have included tolerance and the sound byte culture. In extemporaneous speaking, students tackle such current and controversial questions as, Should civil lawsuits against former Bush administration officials who are accused of excesses in the "War on Terror" be allowed to proceed? Has the federal government gone too far in bailing out failed U.S. businesses? and What can the Mexican government do to secure an edge in the war against drug lords? To succeed in these events, students must have an in-depth understanding of social and political issues. Further, they develop critical thinking skills through their exploration of these issues.

Before competing, students must conduct research on a wide range of topics and compare sources, dissect the quality of the material, and synthesize information from multiple resources. In 1999, a team of collegiate forensics coaches conducted a meta-analysis study of public speaking classes, argumentation classes, and competitive forensics programs that confirmed this analysis. Their research indicated that "all methods of communication skill training improvement generates gains in critical thinking. The largest effect, however, was observed for competitive forensic participation" (Allen, Berkowitz, Hunt, & Louden, 1999).

A Dialectical Approach

The third type of event, debate, meets educational needs as well. Contrary to many assumptions, debate is not a win-at-all-costs activity. At their core, academic debates foster discussions on controversial topics. But, unlike classroom discussions on similar issues, students do not get to pick their side. Students must be prepared to defend multiple sides of the topics. In any given competition, they will fill the affirmative (proposition) and negative (opposition) side of the issue an equal number of times in four, six, or eight preliminary round tournaments. This practice is often referred to as switch-sides debate because competitors are regularly moving from pro to con and back again during each successive round. Their involvement in this activity truly incorporates a dialectal approach to civic education.

Most noticeably, debaters take what they learned and share those ideas in the classroom when they return to school following a tournament. Many of my students have expressed that their interest in a government, philosophy, or science class was sparked at a debate tournament. They have shared their ideas, and those of their competitors, with their classmates in units on constitutional law, the civil rights movement, and the greenhouse effect. As a result, other faculty members and administrators frequently told me how lucky I was to have such bright and talented students on my team. Although my students are bright and talented, I believe these statements oversimplified the reality. The truth is, *all* students are bright. Their teachers just have not reached them yet.

Anecdotal evidence suggests that debaters are much more likely to take a meaningful role in the community as well. Through debate, they learn the importance of ordinary citizens taking an active role in the society in which they live and gain a greater understanding of cultures and governmental systems, thereby increasing their ability to play a meaningful role within those contexts. The discourse that occurs on a debate team between tournaments and at forensics competitions gives debaters a greater understanding of those who are different from themselves, a sense of interconnectedness, and knowledge of how to work more effectively with others. Translating these ideas to the business world, "a number of CEOs and company presidents who have formal debate experience" credited much of their success to the logical thinking and interpersonal skills they developed at debate competitions (Jones, 2004, p. 3B).

Of equal significance, debate fosters discussion among competitors and forces them to consider multiple sides of an issue. In addition, they examine each issue from nonpartisan angles because they must invariably debate both sides of the topic. More importantly, students examine the issues in context, rather than as separate and unrelated topics. They see for themselves that policy discussions in the real world do not occur in a vacuum.

Further, debaters gain the opportunity to examine the interplay of actual policy ideas and alternatives as they apply their research and arguments in an academic laboratory at debate competitions. There, they share their ideas with others in both formal and informal discussions, gain additional insight on the topics from their competitors, and often engage their judges in postround analysis of the subjects and arguments that were debated. Thus, they add yet another layer of depth to their understanding.

Finally, debaters' discussions empower them to develop meaningful arguments through the process of making claims, supporting those claims with facts and evidence, and contributing their own thoughtful analysis. Debaters choose their arguments after synthesizing information from multiple resources, including popular media, history's great philosophers, and government studies and the research of independent think tanks. They necessarily must learn to analyze the quality and credibility of their sources before they create their own arguments and analysis. In fact, a recent study indicated that in urban school settings, academic debate programs have had a positive impact on students' critical reading ability (Collier, 2007). Ultimately, this not only aids their ability to learn in all areas of the curriculum, but it also grows thoughtful and informed citizens.

Conclusion

Forensics—interpretation, speech, and debate—can and should be a meaningful part of every school's curriculum. To put it simply, the course of study, alongside cocurricular competition, promotes civic education and enhances the standard curriculum by helping students explore myriad topics from multiple angles and find the truth in each, fostering civic participation, advocating civic engagement, promoting authentic discussions on issues of real importance, and emphasizing the principles that are essential to a liberal democracy.

REFERENCES

- Allen, M., Berkowitz, S., Hunt, S., & Louden, A. (1999). A meta-analysis of the impact of forensics and communication education on critical thinking [Electronic version]. *Communication Education* 48(1), 18-30.

- Crawford, R. (2003, November). In defense of competitive speech [Electronic version]. *Rostrum*, 78(3). Retrieved on April 15, 2008, from www.nflonline.org/uploads/Rostrum/speechcrawford1103.pdf

- Collier, L. M. (2007, October). NDCA coaches' corner: Studies show high school debate enhances reading: Quantitative studies. *Rostrum*, 82(2), 52-53.

- Jones, D. (2004, September 30). Debating skills come in handy in business. *USA Today*, 3B.

- Martin, J. N., & Nakayama, T. K. (2004). *Intercultural communication in contexts* (3rd ed..). Boston: McGraw-Hill.

- McCrady, R. (2004, November). Forensics, debate, and the SAT. *Rostrum*, 79(3), 41-44.

- Parker, W. C. (2006). Teaching against idiocy. In F. Schultz (Ed.), *Annual editions: Education: Vol. 06/07* (pp. 47-52). Dubuque, IA: McGraw-Hill. (Reprinted from Phi Delta Kappan, pp. 344-351, by W. C. Parker, 2005)

Adventures in Debate: Communication between East and West

By Li Xi (Cecilee)

Lecturer (tenured) at Beijing Foreign Studies University

Why Debate? As I sit down to ponder the question and look into this thought-provoking question, I find my answers are almost the reflection of my thirteen year journey of debate. The glamour of debating and the beauty of thinking behind all it requires, guiding me through my career goal and penetrating almost every aspect of my intellectual life as a student, an educator, and a global citizen.

My introduction to competitive English-language debate

My story is atypical among my peers in China. Parliamentary debate was introduced in China around 2000 and competitive debate has a relatively young history in this nation. My journey of debate coincides with this timeline of development, as my story could almost be viewed as a personal history of how parliamentary debate has flourished in China.

I was among the earliest group of college students on the Chinese mainland who engaged in debate. My former university where I finished my undergraduate studies—Xi'an International Studies University (XISU)—hosted the very first parliamentary debate workshop in China in 2000. Before I was enrolled as an English major in 2002, XISU already hosted several international debates and intercultural exchanges between China and the United States.

Before entering college, I had never heard of parliamentary debate. Out of the love of ancient language and culture, I first started my connection with debating by joining the Chinese debating team as a freshman. Instead of Aristotle, we have Mencius, one of the most known ancient philosophers in China, who is believed to have been a very eloquent persuader. Debating fascinates me as a unique and intense way of communication in my own language. Although not stereotyping debating as a synonym of quarrelling, like a lot of people in my culture may do, I avoid any forms of debating in my daily life, yet look up to those eloquent speakers on the stage who can always defend their opinions or defeat their rivals by words and tactics of using language.

My initial understanding of debating was shallow as I re-flected upon it later, but it directly led me to explore more in the world of English debate. I joined the English-language debate team and attended my first parliamentary workshop in late 2002, with a strong curiosity in discovering how new and different it was from the kind of debate I had already known. At that moment, I was not aware at all that the biggest impact to me during the rest of my college days would be debating in English, and everything it brings beyond the language.

To begin with, debate urges me to think and taught me to reason. In the very early stage, parliamentary debate in China was easily interpreted as a new and demanding extracurricular activity with the expressed purpose of learning English. It mostly began among English majors. Students participating in this activity have a strong incentive to improve their oral English skills, since judges may use similar criteria to adjudicate an English-language debate as an English speech contest, which highlights grammar, pronunciation, manners on the stage, and the fluency of language as important voting issues. Given the interactive nature of debate and the need to think through ideas in both your native and non-native tongue, the activity inherently requires one to really explore and learn the English language. Admittedly, language proficiency is a fine premise to effective communication, but very soon I found that the excitement and demand of this new style of debating far exceeded the purpose of simply learning English.

It is important to have good language and delivery, but it is the ideas that matter most. As an interactive activity, it involves much more impromptu speaking than an English class or speech competition, and heavily relies on evidence and logic. Furthermore, the topics are about current social and world issues, like world energy crisis or reform of education systems, which are not to be found in textbooks or conventional classrooms. A new world of debating was revealed to me. I started to practice regularly and intensely with my teammates, doing research for motions (or debate topics) on different areas and participated in a series of local, intercollegiate, and national tournaments.

Debate also led me to intercultural communication. My first intercultural debate experience happened in the summer vacation before my sophomore year. My school held a one-week international debate festival that hosted over forty American coaches and debaters on campus. The scale was the first of its kind for Chinese mainland universities. Besides being a debater, I was the chief volunteer of this festival, helping organize a workshop, the tournament, and a cultural tour. I had never communicated extensively with so many native English speakers within such a short span of time. But this chance stimulated the best self inside of me at that time, with my limited experience in either debating or intercultural exchange, to be not just a representative of the hosting school, but also a genuine friend and sincere ambassador to introduce my culture and my country to all guests from afar.

I remember I had an intense debate with my Chinese partner against two high school students from New York. In the whip speech, I summarized six points of my opponents' side and deconstructed each one of them with my basic understanding of refutation. As a novice debater, I was surprised that I could speak (*in English*) so fast and talk so much within 5 minutes, a progress I didn't expect before I engaged in debating. It impressed the judge of the debate as well, who gave me advice on grouping ideas but also encouraged me to continue further along the way.

After each debate, it is the handshake and the smiling exchange of friendship first between debaters of both sides that make everything worthwhile. The conversation I had with my American counterparts and judges extended in between and after debates, and moved from campuses to places of interest including Terracotta Warriors, Forest of Stone Tablets, Muslin Street, and Goose Pagoda. The historical and cultural icons of Xi'an—one of the best-preserved ancient capitals in China—saw the growth of the debating community and international friendship through this activity. Later along my journey of debate, I travelled to many tournaments in different places around the world and met many different people. But it all started from this fascinating process of intercultural exchange and my further understanding about why debate—to meet people, to see the world, to establish meaningful connections, and create understanding for yourself and others.

My first journey with western debate

Debate also brought me to the United States for my first international trip. In the summer of 2005, I was fully-sponsored to attend debate camp in Willamette, Oregon, as a reward for winning a regional tournament hosted by XISU in the previous winter. I travelled with three other debaters and two coaches from Xi'an, and we were warmly received by the Willamette debating community, led by Robert Trapp. Later, we learned that we were the first group of Chinese ever to attend this event.

The six of us were divided to join smaller debate groups led by different mentors. After three to four days of systematic training and practice within each group, debaters came back altogether and competed in an ad hoc tournament. Within the small group, I got individualized mentoring like all other members with improved understanding on argumentation, motion analysis, case-construction, team-building, and other relevant strategies of debating. The information was overwhelming, but I fully enjoyed it. As an English as a Foreign Language (EFL) learner, each debate was a leap of my English language skills, as I was debating with and against native English speakers, and my confidence grew little by little through each round. I felt encouraged every time my American group mates gave me a thumb-up or my mentor offered careful individual feedback.

I remember taking notes fiercely for each speech; my mind worked in the same pace to think and organize responses to everything I heard. It is all required to happen simultaneously and without hesitation, thinking simultaneously in my native tongue and in English. I thought, "*I shall be ready to stand up at any point, like a warrior, to defend or challenge with words and reasons.*" It was a mind-blowing experience to me, and I loved it. The debate camp boosted my confidence to compete and cooperate with native English speakers. It also led to a deeper understanding of what makes the best debate—the quality of argument, the depth of engagement, the respect for your opponent, and the spirit to face difficulties and live up to your potential—it is the philosophy of debating that could work on anybody, no matter where you come from or which language you speak.

After the Willamette camp, I went to Los Angeles with my group for another cultural tour. We took Greyhound as our transportation and had a long journey along the West Coast. I remember vividly my excitement of being on the road, sitting long hours inside the bus but not getting bored. It was my first trip to a foreign nation. Furthermore, I had been learning English for more than ten years—including two years' of professional studies at college—but it was the first time I set my foot in an English speaking country.

Although America is heavily studied in China, it was still in veil to me until this trip. Like Columbus or my ancestor Zheng

He, who sailed across the Indian Ocean towards the vast world of unknown 700 years ago, I was on my own journey to the West. I was looking at the changing landscape outside—mountains, forests, orchards, houses, and even cars and animals—observing and thinking about how different or similar this land is with my own country on the other side of the Pacific Ocean. Debate brought me this far to a new continent that I felt amazing and thankful at the same time. On the trip, I chatted with different local people, trying to have a leisure dialogue between the East and the West. I was surprised when a very friendly elder couple asked me if people in China wear ancient costumes—like those in the movie *Hidden Dragon and Crouching Tiger*—in daily life. That seems to be the kind of scene about China in their mind—exotic, mysterious, and everybody knows Kung Fu. I think I may have surprised them, when I told them I never wear such a costume, that most of the people I know don't play any Kung Fu, and everybody learns English. We had a long conversation about our own countries.

Later, in L.A, our group was hosted by Professor Gary Rybold and Irvine Valley College. They organized intercultural activities for us to meet American students and coaches who had travelled and debated in China. The one-week stay in southern California provided me with a scope to look closer into America. This time, the American debaters became our guides, accompanying us to their campuses and places of interest like Hollywood, Laguna Beach, and the Getty Museum. We caught the 50th anniversary of Disneyland, and I was quite surprised to find that most souvenirs in Disney were Made in China. We watched the Shamu Show at Sea World and even sat in a baseball game between the L.A Angels and New York Yankees. I was overwhelmed at the stadium with over 45,000 frenetic audiences, feeling like breaking into a super noisy dream. In the same stadium, I was amazed by how pop music and Christianity can combine together while listening to a Christian rock music concert.

But above all of these culture shocks, I felt my mind and heart lifted for the real face-to-face and heart-to-heart intercultural communication during this trip. One of the American debaters invited the whole China group to her house, as she emphasized, for returning the favor she had once received while she was in China. She and her family prepared us a homemade feast, like a new year's dinner, to treat the oriental stomachs. So we had a grand Thanksgiving feast with turkey and pumpkin pie in the middle of the summer, and everybody ate to our hearts' content. The happiness of this meal went far beyond the tastiness of the food. We voted to name that day a real "thanksgiving" day with full appreciation and gratitude to each other. Without knowing any concept profound or sophisticated about intercultural theories, I knew I had one of the best intercultural experiences in my life.

We are all connected because of debating, but it is a means rather than an end. The power of connection comes from people, and the human interactions, the kindness, and the appreciation of otherness exchanged among people, which helped me to be open-minded and embrace the diversity and unknown possibilities of the world. At the end of the intercultural debate tour, I felt I was indeed refreshed to a new height along my journey. I had crossed a new gateway ready for a bigger world of exploration.

Intercultural immersion in debate

A bigger world did extend itself in front of me. After getting back to Xi'an, I filled the rest of my college days attending every speech and debate tournament I could at local, provincial, or national levels. Together with my teammates, we brought honor and experiences back to campus, helped build a local debating community, and organized further regional and international debates. Unexpectedly, Steve Johnson of the Seawolf Debate team at the University of Alaska Anchorage (UAA) offered me a full debate scholarship upon my graduation, inviting me to continue debating in the U.S. while studying for a master's degree in rhetoric.

From many documentaries and novels we may find, Alaska is a legendary place. Bear Grylls and Barrack Obama both had their adventures there. For a lot of people who have never been, this is the place for running wild, not debating. For me, Alaska is like an adventure, but in a very different way. The breathtaking landscape did fuel my love of nature, but instead of wilderness, bears, or northern lights, it was the rigorous academic training in both my master's program and debate that makes it a truly exceptional experience to me. As there were few graduate students from the Chinese mainland at UAA at that time, it was a wonderland of total English and cultural immersion.

I should admit, it was very challenging for me at the very beginning. Although located far from the "Lower 48," Alaska has one of the most active debating societies in the U.S. The team travels extensively to different parts of North America and around the world for tournaments. Being the first international member of the team, I felt honored as well as pressured. The team participates in British Parliamentary (BP) debate, which was a different format than the American format first intro-duced to China. The motions of daily practice had a lot to do with current world or American issues, like international relations, foreign policy, or legislation, which I was unfamiliar with while debating in China.

Furthermore, it was very demanding for me to cope with the heavy workload of my major studies and the intense training on the debate team at the same time. My coach and teammates were all very nice and helpful, but in a team where there were national champions and best speakers, I knew there was still a great deal to catch up with my fellow teammates. Nonetheless, I cherished this rare and extremely valuable opportunity to learn. Every week, the team gathered twice at the squad room for long hours of practice and training. I remember I ran between classrooms and squad room for most of the school days, and stayed up late to work on debate briefs as well as course papers.

After the initial period of frustration, I stretched every brain cell and tuned in the antenna inside me to receive and digest all sorts of information, communicating extensively with my professors, classmates, and team members to adapt to this new environment.

For two years, I travelled with my teammates to debate in different locations around the U.S. In most of the tournaments, I was the only Asian face. I did not feel like a minority though, as gradually language was no longer a barrier for me. I was able to think in English and spoke fluently and clearly most of time, like a native English speaker. I went through almost a hundred rounds of debate and observed even more, as I integrated myself fully to this argumentative culture. However, I have never forgotten my own identity and origin.

Being a bilingual debater, I had the valuable experiences to have debated extensively in both China and the United States, which gave me a unique perspective to observe and reflect upon the differences between the two cultures. In the tranquility and even solitude of my days in Alaska, I had a lot of time to reflect upon the nature of debate. When I put myself as an outsider of the West, I found debating is indeed one of the best ways to understand the western mindset, which is distinctively different from the way of thinking I had been familiar with.

In Chinese culture, people tend to avoid conflicts. Debate, seeming like a quarrel and containing tit-for-tat verbal disagreement, could be unpleasant to think about in the first place. Like Master Oogway in *Kung Fu Panda*, Chinese minds like to put the ideas or messages in high-context language, sometimes very implicitly, like a riddle, that the receivers must read between the lines.

The linear way of being direct might not always be a desirable feature in communication, and it might not be the strategy on the top of the list for resolving conflicts or disputes. There is a saying in Chinese: "seek the commonality and put the differences aside," which reflects the philosophy of harmony in the oriental value system. The Chinese way of achieving harmony tends to avoid conflict in the first place, and if possible—"resolve big disputes to small ones; resolve small ones to none." On the contrary, the western way of realizing harmony is to put the conflict on the table, tear it down openly, transparently, and sometimes fiercely about all the relevant aspects before a final voting or decision is made.

Parliamentary debate is a miniature of this way of thinking, and I could see it in every motion I debated. Jumping out of the academic arena at schools, debate is a widely applicable approach to resolve problems in the real world. It could be a form to help settle upon a policy in Congress or elect a presidential candidate. It could be a step to process a criminal case at court. For ordinary people, it could be a way to hear different opinions, to make their own voices empowered for rational civic engagement.

Still, the understanding of why we debate may differ from person to person. But the more I ponder upon the essence of debating, the more I understand why it has been so prevalent in western society, and why sometimes the dialogue between the East and the West may be difficult—because of the inherent differences in the two systems of thinking and communication. At other times, stereotypes and misunderstanding may occur because of different beliefs or stances, or simply because of a lack of communication.

I remember in one debate, my opponent challenged my understanding of rights and liberty because I come from, as I quote, "a nation of communism." I was shocked, rather than offended. I realized how people's perceptions may be shaped by things they don't exactly see or know, or are shaped in different ways because of different sources of information.

Debate gave an opportunity for constructive dialogue. I took the challenge and shared my own stories with my audience as a living example of life in China. I grew up in an ordinary but loving family, received my higher education, and had frequent but safe travels inside my own country. Like most of my peers, I never felt starvation, threat, or prosecution of any kind in my life. I may not know my country in every aspect, but I know it as a fast-developing land for life, opportunities, and choices, which is much more alive than a rigid label of ideology.

Later, I learned none of the people sitting in the round had ever been to China, which is fully understandable given the geographic distance. Still, I advised my audience to take a trip to China if possible, like I have traveled to the United States, to discover more than what I can personally describe before drawing a conclusion. We may still disagree with each other at some point and don't have to see things in the same way, but at least our judgment could be based more upon our own empirical observations. I am not sure whether my words may work, but at least debate provided a platform for us to hear different voices, which could set us all into more thinking.

Debate broke my own stereotype, as well. In one of the early debates I had in Alaska, there was a motion about whether the U.S. should boycott products that are Made in China. The context of the motion involved an incident in the summer of 2007 that a large quantity of toys coming out of China were recalled for containing toxic levels of lead paint. It was a shameful pity for me to see the incident happened, as I understand safety should be the priority for children's toys, and the ethics of production should be upheld in any trade.

Yet, I still felt reluctant at the beginning to debate this motion—I am sort of Made in China, as well. It sounded like putting the whole export industry as a scapegoat for this one incident; a deliberate antagonism out of sentiment that could harm consumers and producers in both nations. I could be right or wrong personally, but it was also through this discussion, I got two important messages about debate. One is that by debating any motion, whether you personally agree or not, it does not mean to push ideas or alter beliefs. The positions are randomly chosen that you shall prepare to speak for any speaker's role, and every motion, like a coin, has two sides. Your ability to argue rationally despite of your disagreement marks your degree of empathy, an important sign of maturity as a compassionate human being. Second, scrutiny is one of the best lessons to learn. Whether for a nation or an individual, we should have the strength to face scrutiny, sometimes accompanied with crisis, to examine ourselves, to distinguish deliberate rivalry from objective criticism, and take actions to strive for better.

The more I debated, the more I realized that the special contribution, if I could make any, whether in debating or in daily communication, is to be an ambassador to bridge more understanding across cultures. East or West, there is wisdom and legacy passed down through generations. I may not be able to resolve big world conflicts, but by establishing an effective two-way communication with people around me, I may still bring small but good changes to this world, or at least to my community. Through debating and all these meaningful intercultural exchanges, the world became small as well as big to me. The UAA and Anchorage community embraced me with its legends and made my adventures in Alaska part of it too. When I first started my journey of debating, I didn't anticipate that it would lead me so far to see so many things along the way. The pursuit of intellectualism is a life-long career. With the help of everything I learned through debate, I shall keep walking, to embrace more possibilities in my journey.

Li Xi (Cecilee), currently teaching at Beijing Foreign Studies University (BFSU), was one of the earliest parliamentary debaters and debate educators on the Chinese mainland. She served a leading role in the Chinese debating community by being the Chief Adjudicator in a series of national and international debating tournaments in China, including the EU-China International Tournament, the BFSU-International Debate Education Association national tournament, and the FLTRP Cup (China's English-language national debate championship). She served as China's Representative to the World Universities Debating Championship Annual Council from 2009 to 2011. She has travelled extensively to numerous tournaments as an invited adjudicator, including the U.S. Universities Debating Championship and the Hobart & William Smith Colleges Round Robin. She is a steadfast promoter of intercultural communication and innovator in critical thinking education. She designed and teaches the first English-language debate course as part of the compulsory curriculum for non-English Majors in China.

Not a Team, but a Family

By Nicole Maria Eldred

Student at William & Lee University

Forensics (or speech and debate) from the outside looks like a bunch of kids dressed in fancy clothes, speaking really fast, and that spend hours and hours researching things that most people care nothing about. From the inside, it looks pretty much the same. You spend hours perfecting your arguments and cases. Spend more money on coffee than you would a new computer. Focus more attention on your debate case than your AP exams. Not to mention stressing about whether or not your suit jacket matches your suit pants, or if your dress is too short. You count wmp (the rate at which words flow from your mouth each minute), because you have to make every second count. Sometimes you even have competitions for the highest wmp. The difference? From the inside you know that the looks are just scraping the surface of the activity.

Not every person is popular, sporty, or accepted by everyone. Especially in high school, that can be very difficult. There are the nerds, dorks, athletes, high achievers, popular kids, outcasts, and many, many others. Each debater is their own person, just like everyone else. And just like every group or clique, forensics attracted all sorts of people. The most amazing thing was that it did not matter if you were prom king (yes, we had a couple on the team), president of the National Honor Society (for four straight years all NHS presidents were forensic members), star basketball player, or Dungeons and Dragons fanatic. Everyone was accepted and loved for who they were.

Years after graduating and leaving the forensics world behind, the memories and friends still linger. Most of the people I still keep in touch with from high school were on the debate team. Because they were not just friends, they were family.

When I started high school I was facing a rough transition. Life was a surreal blur. I never knew how to really say what I was feeling. I never really had anyone with whom I could articulate the turmoil within me. I was an awkward freshman looking for somebody to take me under his or her wing. Or in my case, somebodies.

Shawn Briscoe (my coach at the time and the lead author of this book, honestly is one of the reasons I am the person I am today) was the mother of the debaters, of our team. He had the poise to make us want to hold our tongues, the gaiety to keep us entertained, the tenderness to make us feel safe, and most of all the presence to keep us from wanting to disappoint him. Everyone on the team emulated him, however, he wasn't the only one with those qualities. Every debater I have encountered (with the exception of a few lollipops) were kind, sensitive, competitive, and helpful. It was under the guidance of Briscoe that I found what was missing in my life. Debate. And *every hidden meaning* behind the word. He was the one that taught me what it meant to be a debater. However, the most important thing he taught me was how to be a person.

Debate helped me figure out who I wanted to be, and the people I wanted to surround myself with. The older members on the team showed me how to grow from a spastic freshman to a well-spoken spastic freshman. I learned how to speak my mind without fear, and without excess. Rather than relying on my phone to communicate with friends and notes to talk to classmates, I was able to develop my speech to talk to people, like a normal person. Debate turned a shy and stuttering girl into someone who could clearly communicate her thoughts. I was able to give speeches at fundraising events, lead groups of people, and speak in class. My grades skyrocketed and my facial muscles grew in size as I smiled more than I had in my entire life.

Now, it wasn't all rainbows and unicorns. My first debate was scary; I was quaking in my boots. I thought I was going to throw up. (*Side note: after one debate I actually threw up.*) I lost. Horribly. So horribly that I wanted to quit. However, I didn't. Because what debate had shown me was worth more than the pride that was damaged. Debate showed me that I could overcome fear. In fact, my father always tells me that he wishes he had learned how to speak in public and speak to people while understanding all sides of an argument.

That first debate, I thought I was all alone. I wasn't, though. As I sat looking at the crowd of faces, I saw that I was supported. I had only just joined the team, and found my entire squad there to support me. Debate is an individual activity; you are competing against everyone, even your own teammates. However, when it comes down to it, the winning isn't the most important thing. The most important thing is being there for one another and supporting each other.

It was that support that I had been lacking in other avenues of my life. I wanted a group of people that was going to support me no matter what. That is what debate is. It is a group of people that want you to succeed, to learn, to make friends, and to have fun. The support doesn't start and end with your squad. It starts the first time you show up to practice and ends with the writing on your tombstone.

I have attended competitions all over the United States, and continue to find that people are always willing to help one another. I am still in contact with teams from across the nation, helping them improve their cases and working with them on case strategy. When I was still debating, they provided the same support for me. Yes, everyone wants to win, and yes, winning is nice. I would be a liar if I said I didn't get satisfaction from winning. But winning never meant anything if it meant I had to sacrifice my friendship or win at the expense of others. By helping one another we all got better. We worked together to ensure mutual success. I can't remember how many hours and times I shared information with teammates that not only made us better debaters, but also made the circuit better as a whole.

It wasn't just about helping teammates; it was about making sure everyone felt the same support that you did. Debate is one of the most important things in my life and has taught me not only invaluable life-lessons but has helped to uncover things about myself that I never knew. I want other people to understand what an impact debate can make on your life, if only you let it.

One of the most defining moments in my debate career was at a tournament a couple years ago. While at this tournament, two coaches from different high schools approached me to ask favors. The first coach asked if I would be willing to work with one of her students to help him with debate. This student had not had a lot of success thus far and the coach informed me that I was someone her student looked up to and wanted to learn from. I was flattered; I had never thought of myself as someone that other people looked up to for guidance.

The second coach that approached me asked if her students could watch my next debate. She felt that they could learn a lot from watching my round and studying my debate style. I was once again flattered and honored by her request and readily agreed. I was excited for the opportunity to share something I was so passionate about.

After their students watched my next debate, I took them aside and went over the debate round step by step. I discussed the round with them to see what they thought of it, and what they would have done if they had been in my shoes. At the next tournament, I saw the result of this experience as the students won their debate, and ran to me, thanking me for my help. After that, I watched the two student's rounds and was amazed at how well they were able to argue. It was inspiring to see how much of a difference a little help and confidence could make. Rather than fear, I saw excitement and joy in these students' eyes as they met their opponent head on. That sort of reaction is something I want to see from everyone in the debate community, see them realize that it isn't just about winning. It is about learning and having fun, and when you do both of those, you have succeeded. I am not the only person that feels that way. I saw it time and time again on every circuit, in every state, all over the nation. Winning was fun, but succeeding and sharing that success was better.

Granted, sometimes it is difficult to separate the competitiveness of debate from the fun side of forensics, the bonds between teammates, and the friendship. I mean, who would show up to a forensics tournament wanting to come in second best? The answer for most everyone is, *not me*. I frequently hear horror stories of cutthroat teams that refuse to talk to the competition or are downright hostile to them. I have faced it myself when traveling for debate, seen the ruthless personalities. However, I urge you to learn from a secluded circuit that embodies what forensics should be, a circuit that I hope everyone has the chance to experience at some point in their forensics lives.

For this little lay circuit in Anchorage, Alaska, nothing is more important than growing the circuit, making friends, and encouraging our little sport to grow in numbers. I know this isn't unique to Alaska; it is just my experience. Take it from us, to be competitive and successful, you don't have to be ruthless; you can be kind, sharing, and helpful, and reach the same level of success.

Often, it took traveling home to Alaska to recognize how much we learned from the tournaments. It took those long flights home to gain a little perspective about the nature of the tournament, the personalities we had faced, and what was truly important. In fact, I have had some of the worst and best experiences on flights with my team, both before and after these tournaments. I have seen my coach curled up on a bench with a Snuggie and two pillow pets (none were his); I've spent fourteen hours talking about debate; I've missed flights, been delayed for six hours, and been rerouted all over the country.

Four years, four nationals, four national circuit tournaments, three new coaches, two state tournaments, and enough memories to last a lifetime. It is crazy to think about all the people I met, once or twice, or saw every tournament. It is insane to think that my debate career is over. However, I then think about how it is not over. My debate career will never be over. I will never be able to unlearn the things that debate taught me, or forget the people I have met and the experiences we all shared. I have cried tears of joy, happiness, sadness, and excitement. I have laughed until I cried, and laughed from sheer sleep deprivation. I have pulled pranks on coaches, teammates, and friends. Debate is not just something that you do to pad a resume or learn how to argue. It is about gaining a new perspective on your own life.

I joined the debate team in the hopes that I could find people to which I could relate. What I found was not that. *I found a family.* I found people that I could rely on for anything, from boy troubles, to tutoring, to help with college applications. They are not just people. They are relatives that would do anything for me, rain or shine, no questions asked. When you join debate, you don't do it for the wins and the trophies. You do it for the memories and for the people. You do it to be part of something bigger than yourself.

Nicole Eldred is a sophomore at William & Lee University. Although not debating in college, she participated in Lincoln-Douglas debate, congressional debate, policy debate, public forum, domestic extemporaneous speaking, extemporaneous commentary, and dramatic interpretation of literature in high school. Nicole is an avid advocate for animal and human rights. Currently, she is working to eliminate the need for poaching in nations with poaching issues. She is working to increase the standard of living in these nations so that poaching is no longer needed as a source of income. She hopes her efforts will help both communities and animals in those areas.

The Speaker in the Blue Agbada: What Debate Is For Me

By Richard Omoniyi-Shoyoola

Student at the University of Chicago

Policy debate is an activity able to awaken the highest of skills within a student. It starts from critical thinking and analysis of real world scenarios, then shifts to an understanding of the unique role that one plays within the world around them, and lastly reveals the power one has to become an advocate for the issues they love and care about, making a lasting impact upon the world. In my opinion, it is one of high school's hidden gems, as it carries the blueprints for future world leaders to find themselves and emerge to do incredible things.

I had the fortune of being a policy debater for Metro Academic and Classical High School in St. Louis, and I believe that my journey as a debater speaks to the benefits of this activity. From the beginning of my debating career to the end, I found myself thinking critically about the world around me in case writing, expressing myself and developing my character at tournaments, as well as taking the skills I'd learned forward to be active in my community.

Debate really started for me at the very beginning of my freshman year, on the first day of school. Every club and organization was advertising themselves to the student body in the auditorium onstage, and I was really intrigued by what I had heard from one of the varsity debaters named Julia. Julia was an accomplished debater, having competed at the national tournaments twice. Looking back, I can say that I found myself intimidated by her success. I never imagined that I'd be able to make it as far as she did. When she talked about how debate was an activity that broadens horizons, develops speaking skills, and earns you honorable awards, I honestly fell in love. I approached her to learn more about the activity. She explained to me how debate would be hard work, but that it truly pays off. Still nervous about my abilities, I was resolved to face the challenge. I realized that this was something that I really wanted to do.

Debate isn't an activity that rewards laziness or unoriginality. In every round, debaters find themselves confronted with unique arguments on the spot; arguments that even hours of discussions at team practices fail to foresee. Additionally, you have to defend against those unique arguments, pinpointing flaws in your opponents' points that they may have forgotten, not adequately prepared to defend, or overlooked during their own preparation efforts.

After I joined the team, I learned this quickly. My partner and I learned how to cultivate our cases; freshman year's topic was about space exploration, sophomore year it was about our nation's transportation infrastructure, and so forth. We spent time in the library studying, reading, and cutting cards (or preparing evidence) we felt would help us in debate rounds. This is what debate became for me. It was like adding another class to my schedule, but it quickly grew into something I poured my heart and soul into. I began to grow personally invested in the arguments we made, as if we were actual policymakers making a case before Congress. I will never forget the subtle sadness I felt at the end of each debate year as I looked back to the collection of files I had amassed, never to be used again.

Moving into junior year, I found myself having grown familiar with the analytics and critical thinking that debate helped cultivate within my own patterns of thought. My experiences with debate took on a new character, becoming less of an extracurricular activity and more of a personal delight. This journey of mine had a significant impact upon me outside of debate rounds as well. As a result of all of my experiences, I had grown comfortable with debate, but I was still in need of the character developments it provides. The opportunity to develop these key traits arose during the City Championship tournament of my junior year.

I boldly decided to compete in this particular tournament, while dressed in full traditional Nigerian *agbada*. I wore a bright blue *buba* (a long shirt) and *sokoto* (long pants). I was resolved to make an impression through an expression of my Nigerian heritage. While competing that day, my new partner, Mary and I failed to attain what we had so passionately pursued: a first place plaque and ticket to the national tournament in Washington, D.C. Instead, I found myself at the culmination of an incredibly rewarding journey, having learned much about my character. Walking in, I was a proud debater, certain that the day would end in success. I found myself in debate rounds growing eager to win, subtly losing sight of the educational benefits of the activity. "*Nationals!*" The thought was swimming through my mind, and I was drifting away from the core of what debate is about.

Debate, in addition to being an activity that develops one's critical thinking abilities, also develops one's character. Whether looking at the discipline required consistently taking time out of one's schedule and preparing for rounds or simply respecting an opposing team's arguments and positions, it cultivated the grace one develops when a round fought hard for is lost. All of these things come together to forge within a student unique attributes. The thing that makes them unique is that they specifically help make this person into a more capable leader. That day, at the Soldan High School tournament, I learned an important lesson about myself. My cultivated discipline, humility, and grace were all virtues that could not be overlooked or undervalued. Debate enabled me to see this for the truth that it is.

While at this City Championship tournament Mary and I finished in third place overall, I went home having learned a powerful lesson on the role that I play as a debater. It's more than my win/loss record. The debate round is a meeting of the minds— a place for a young person to engage with others and learn more about their own ways of thinking. The successes are opportunities to showcase the benefits within one's own ideas, while the losses are times to reflect upon the flaws in an argument and improve upon them. The two are equally significant, since both make the other more impactful and inspiring.

As senior year approached, Mary and I developed our resolve to do better at debate tournaments and make it to nationals. We fought hard over the course of the season, doing our best to stay humble while passionately developing new arguments. We won tournament after tournament, until the City Championship arrived once again. Understanding the importance of winning with humility and enjoying the journey, the two of us were undefeated competitors, and doubly qualified for the national tournament. It was the most proud I have felt in a long time, and as I look back I can say that it was definitely one of the highlights of my senior year. This is proof of the transformative power that debate can have upon a person. Could that young freshman boy I once was, nervous about joining the debate team, ever have imagined the journey upon which he would be embarking?

This journey has carried me farther in life. I served as an intern for Mayor Francis Slay of St. Louis, under whom I edited appointment letters, assisted constituents who called the office, and worked to help develop the city's Food Truck infrastructure projects. Debate instilled in me a dedication and passion to make the world a better place, made it easier for me to understand the value in public service and public relations. I served under the Student Advisory Board of the Superintendent of the St. Louis Public Schools [district], and helped to provide key insights about the concerns and needs of students at my high school. In so doing, I learned the importance of responding to the needs and desires of the everyday person, echoing the public advocacy I took part in as a debater.

Through debate I was also introduced to the valuable role that teamwork plays in public affairs, and that when people unite to help others, they go farther and accomplish more. The hours spent working with a partner cemented these notions within my mind, and I was able to apply these ways of thinking to the new opportunities that presented themselves to me.

As a current student at the University of Chicago, where I am now studying political science and public policy, I have had the fortune of meeting and engaging with public officials and leaders of community outreach organizations. I ask them about their commitments to the people of our country, the benefits of their proposals, the strategies they hope to utilize—much like the cross-examination that occurs within debates. I even hope to one day run for public office myself, where I believe I can best use my talents to be a blessing in the lives of others, fighting to make their voices heard. Without having had humility, social awareness, and critical thinking instilled within me through debate, I'm not certain of how ready I would be to be the advocate that my country needs. In many ways, debate contained the first steps of what will be an incredible journey for me, and each day I find myself falling in love with it anew. Who knows what life holds around the corner? Could I even imagine?

Richard Omoniyi-Shoyoola is an aspiring public official from St. Louis, Missouri, and is currently attending the University of Chicago. He enjoys watching The Young Turks' online broadcasts and reading Cracked.com articles. He is proud of his Nigerian heritage and thinks being black is a beautiful thing. A big fan of Chinua Achebe and Chimamanda Ngozi Adichie, Richard also wishes to one day publish his own novels. For speaker engagements, please contact Richard at romoniyishoyoola@gmail.com.

A Path to Adulthood

By Kenny Hubbell

Student at Princeton University

I joined my high school debate team at the beginning of my sophomore year. I was motivated by a half-truth told to a girl from summer camp—that I was "becoming involved with the debate team"—while trying to seem more interesting. Joining the team was one of the best decisions I've ever made. Sometimes I'm asked if I liked debate, or what it was like. It is an impossible project to totally describe my experience with that team.

Internally, I'm limited by a cycle of nostalgia and complicated memories when I try to detail my experiences in those years. Externally, to fully explain my time with that team would require me to explain the process of growing up. How do you describe the feeling of having your name called to participate in a championship round when it seems like the most important thing in the world to you? How do you describe the feeling of sitting with teammates, bickering like family, and realizing you've found something even more important? Of working and travelling and competing and *building* with these people a sense of belonging that you've never quite had before? Explaining those moments is beyond me, although most people probably recognize them in some form from their own life. So when asked about debate, I talk about two things that define high school for lots of people: academics and friends.

From an academic standpoint, debate was invaluable. Debate taught me to research, to pick out the weaknesses in articles, and to speak with (often feigned) confidence. Those skills continue to serve me every day. There are also add-ons, additional perks of an activity that offer something more fundamental: It trains you to make an argument. Four years out of high school, I still compose papers, reports, and presentations by working through the same patterns of thought that I picked up in debate. *What's the problem that I'm going to talk about? Why hasn't it been fixed? What needs to be done to fix it, and how can I prove that those steps will work?* Maybe most important of all: *Could I summarize the core of this to someone in 30 frantic seconds as my speech ends?* At the most basic level, speech and debate gives high schoolers a chance to practice that critical skill of surveying a tangle of internal thoughts and packaging them into a clear, compelling structure to share with the outside world.

Should convicted felons be allowed to vote? Debaters get hit with topics like this repeatedly. Each time they see one, the research and consideration begins. How many felons are there? Would their votes make a difference? Why do we bar them from voting? Why do we deny them freedoms in general? Punishment? Retribution? Deterrence? Justice? Something else? Which of these purposes are served by the prohibition on voting? I remember wandering into this cloud of ideas in the second topic I debated, and being overwhelmed by all the things that I could say. I remember bouncing fragments of arguments back and forth with teammates. In the end, I remember being forced to sit down, cull through all the exciting ideas in my head, and put together something that I could outline on a 3-by-5 card and summarize in a few sentences. That experience isn't unique to debate—high school and higher education is filled with assignments that force students to put together a coherent thesis—but for me, debate provided a uniquely dense form of practice.

In high school, I would write a paper every two weeks or so for one class or another. Even in the era of multiple choice tests, we were still required to put together an original position from time to time. In debate, I would write some form of self-contained argument at least once a week (a case, a disadvantage, a frontline, an advantage: debaters will recognize the jargon). Every week, I would *also* have multiple debate rounds, either at practice or tournaments. And in each round, I would be confronted with several novel and unexpected arguments that required me to come up with novel and unexpected responses—delivered in simple terms in three to eight minute speeches. I would guess that for every major act of synthetic thinking that was required of me in school, I was driven to perform five for the speech and debate team.

In college, I'll frequently find myself in classroom discussions where, when it comes time to participate and discuss a reading, I'll go through the familiar mental shuffle of lining up two or three observations that support a broader claim. That moment doesn't recall memories of sitting at my desk for an English paper or writing a response essay for a history test. It feels like one of the countless adrenaline-packed moments that I had in debate rounds when I needed to take the fifty "facts" the judge had heard and distill them into one coherent story that supported my team.

Meanwhile, in my life outside of school, I'll find myself wrestling with decisions: Do I apply to medical school next year or take two years off? Do I look for jobs on the East Coast or the West? I break down these questions the way I would a case in debate. Like most people, I think in terms of pros and cons, but I find that the way I balance these arguments against each other is reminiscent of the thinking I'd do for debate:

Claim: The extra year away from school might make it harder to return to studying.

Counter: The extra year of shadowing a doctor will make me more confident in my decision, driving me to work harder in med school.

Claim: The extra year of working lets me save up for school expenses.

Counter: The extra year with a doctor's salary would compensate in the long run.

Again, I don't think the ability to think through personal decisions is something that I wouldn't have figured out without debate. However, debate *did* make careful back-and-forth thinking a habit for me. So when I do make a choice, I feel I've made it with the same well-reasoned analysis that would have won a debate round. And that's a reassuring feeling.

In short, debate was a highly accelerated way to practice the sort of well-organized thinking and communication that improves virtually every piece of academic work and personal decision-making that I've done since. That fundamental skill, beyond all the confidence and facts and rhetorical tricks that I picked up, has served me in my life since.

Debate also taught me to empathize with others' perspectives, making my worldview more flexible. The strongest convictions of my life were those that I held at age fourteen, when I realized that my liberal middle-class vaguely Methodist worldview was *exactly* right. I had never had such passionate, uncomplicated thoughts about any issue, from gun control to school attendance policy, as I did then. And I haven't since. Because of course, I went through the sort of growth that we hope all citizens go through. It would be easy to give debate the credit for that. I could claim that I researched the facts on so many controversial issues, and spent so much time studying their complexities that I emerged perfectly well-informed. But that's ridiculous. I have blind spots on all sorts of things. I don't really understand the resistance to prison reform measures. I don't understand my university's fire code policy. Debate didn't teach me anything about those issues.

What debate made me do was to spend countless hours getting into the heads of people who I disagreed with. I spent at least a quarter of my junior year debate rounds arguing that programs reducing poverty in the U.S. would reduce military recruitment, thereby weakening our military at a critical time. That's a despicable view. I thought so then, and I continue to think so. But I spent enough time defending it that I can imagine the type of person who might think that way. I can even empathize with parts of them—the feeling of insecurity, the sense that the military is a preferable path to work your way out of poverty than a government intervention, and so forth.

The practice of representing the opposing side left me with something better than a balanced view on a selection of controversies. Instead, I left with a more general framework: a willingness to *really listen* to another's argument, to give it full charity, and to work to understand its adherents. In debate that attitude was critical, both to giving a convincing speech on something you didn't actually believe, and to predict an opponent's moves.

In my life since, that attitude has left me someone who is willing to sit down with someone to understand why they're worried about lifting mandatory sentencing laws. I'm someone who understands that somewhere out there is a fire marshal with excellent reasons for the rules about posters on dorm-room doors. And in my classes, when I hear someone make an argument, I can open myself up to be convinced by it—even if it runs counter to my original beliefs.

Conveniently, as it was a voluntary extracurricular, debate was also extremely fun. While it seems natural at this point to think of debate as more fun than work, I understand how it could sound dull. Or terrifying. On paper it sounds like a juried festival of oral reports. So why was debate the best part of my high school weekends?

There's the competitive aspect. Debate was my chance to discover what people who had been seriously playing sports already knew—it was thrilling to go into something, put up the best fight I could, and be rewarded for doing well. And the chance of not doing well just made it all the more exciting. There was an element of personal success as well. It felt good to do well at something, and knowing that I was good at something created a sense of security, confidence, and status that could be addictive. Then there was the biggest part: the people.

The speech and debate team *was* the people. I found a group of friends there that defined high school for me. The debate team was a space where it was safe to be excited about current affairs and social controversies and philosophy. In high school, being enthusiastic about academics often labeled you: nerdy, stuck-up, or know-it-all. But on the debate team, a love of ideas and intellectual exploration wasn't just accepted; it was encouraged as a central value.

People that would never have spoken in a classroom would stand up to give *speeches* on their interpretation of Kant or their recommendations on foreign policy. Others, who spoke vigorously in classroom settings (and I was one of them) would be listened to and challenged on their ideas in a way that rarely happened in the classroom. Not surprisingly, I, and many others on the team, opened up in a way that we had never felt comfortable doing in school. Coming out of your shell, developing a sense of yourself, learning to play well with others—whatever you want to call it, it happened to us in the enclave of speech and debate. The teenage years are the time when we learn a lot about how to get along with each other, and for me, a lot of that socialization happened on the debate team, where I was comfortable being my nerdy, academic, goofy self with some of the best friends I've ever had.

And they are that. We were a group of friends who started playing pranks on each other, and talking through crushes with each other. We learned to drive, and experienced the freedom of driving around town without parents. We spent our summers together, both at national debate tournaments and at each other's houses—making ice cream and stupid movies and jumping on trampolines. We grew up together.

Now, five years since I debated in a tournament with these people, a number of them are still among my closest friends. I can't promise that joining the debate team will make someone happy, or well adjusted, or that it will automatically build friendships. Those are all things that people do for themselves. I can say that for me, it was easier to grow in an environment that made safe all sorts of personality quirks and interests. Maybe it's the nature of debate, which requires that its participants alternate between defending both sides of an issue, that it fosters an environment of acceptance. Or the reverse may be true—in order to develop competitive debaters, experienced coaches encourage an attitude of open-mindedness. Whatever the reason, the debate team was for me—and I suspect many others—a safe place to do the identity-forming work that is central to teenage years.

I'm writing this in my senior year of college as a Chemical and Biological Engineer. I live some four thousand miles from my high school and study protein engineering. I haven't been in a debate for five years. But every few months, I'll be in a seminar and I'll find myself making an argument structured around the difference between *necessary* and *sufficient*. Every few weeks, I'll make some bizarre joke that's met with blank looks, and I'll find myself loving the fact that I'm comfortable doing that. And of course, every few days, I'll text one of my high school debate friends for advice, or to catch up, or just complain about something that I don't want to dump on my local friends. High school debate was three incredibly rich years of life for me, and while I can't describe that experience in its totality, I continue to see its fingerprints on every day of my life.

Kenny Hubbell debated at South Anchorage High School in his sophomore, junior, and senior years. After accepting admission to Princeton University, he spent a school-sponsored gap year interning in Peru. He is a member of Princeton class of 2016, where he studies Chemical Engineering with minors in Global Health and Engineering Biology. While he no longer debates in college, he fills his free time with ceramic arts, backpacking, and cooking projects. After graduation, he will join the pharmaceutical company Merck as a biological engineer.

Section III: Career & Professional Life

Debate was the single most important thing I did in high school or college.

High school debate did more to prepare me for the rigors of college than any class, activity, or leadership position. It taught me how to think critically about any issue. It taught me how to organize my thoughts. It taught me how to present my ideas in a compelling manner. It taught me how to communicate effectively with others.

College debate had a tremendous impact on preparing me for the workforce and professional life. Debate taught me how to see multiple perspectives. It helped me understand the perspective of others. It taught me to respect those perspectives. It helped me to see how multiple lines of reasoning can be combined into a coherent picture in order to pursue a better course of action.

The essays in this section capture the stories of a diverse group of professionals, reflecting on how debate shaped their lives and prepared them for their chosen careers.

Trial By (Academic) Combat

By Jonathon Sanchez

Attorney At Law

Some people will laugh at the premise that debate is inherently a *violent* thing. Here, I posit just that: Debate is *inherently violent*, as in, there is no possible way to conduct debate without violence. The greater academic debate community steadfastly protects and encourages the pillars of modern liberal democracies of reasoned dialogue and rational public discourse. They will agree with Mahatma Gandhi, who is attributed as saying, "honest disagreement is often a good sign of progress." To the chagrin of the academic debate community, and perhaps even to Mr. Gandhi himself, I vehemently encourage others to enlist in the violent activity of debate because it shaped the person I am. Indeed, just as exercise is violent, debate's assault of wits and battle of logic will ultimately strengthen a person's courage, strengthen a person's analytical ability, and even shape a person's inner morality.

You might be surprised to learn that the etymology of debate comes from an Old French word, *debatre*, which translates literally into "to beat down." Ah-ha, so perhaps I am not far off from my word choice (Gandhi be damned!). People underestimate how deeply engrained the need to belong to a group is; indeed, the human desire to belong has biological evidence to back it up. In many ways, disagreement and discord provide a mental violence that goes against a person's need to belong because it disrupts the social order.

Synonyms to debate include dissension, strife, quarrelling, and controversy. In addition, it is generally conducted by and against an adversary or an opponent or the like. This inner stress is exacerbated in the context of competitive college debate since it places this mental turmoil into a tournament setting. Teams are rank-ordered by objective third parties, over the course of a tournament and debate season. The incentive for doing well in the minds of these third parties is scholarship money, prestige, invitations to judge when you retire from competitive debate, travel, a resume line item, groupies, and accolades! Despite these potential benefits, why do people do something that goes against human nature at its core? After all, none of those incentives are guarantees; in fact, failure to achieve those incentives is actually more likely. Well, debaters are crazy, but I can explain what it did for me.

Debate forged the courage that I have today. Prior to debate, I was a very shy, fearful, and socially anxious person. My anxiety hindered my ability to speak clearly. The more others struggled to understand me, the more I did not want to speak. It became a mental feedback loop where the anxiety compounded over time. Locked in my own thoughts, I grew more frustrated because I could not communicate the richness of my inner thoughts.

Time and time again, I held my tongue out of fear that I would embarrass myself. My school and parents believed that perhaps my inability to communicate was because I did not know how to speak, so I spent many monotonous hours in school-mandated speech classes. This trickled into other areas of my life as I grew up, from the mundane to the significant. For example, I was the kind of person who would order something easier to say at a restaurant, rather than what I really wanted. Slowly, my speaking ability improved over my academic career.

Remember in high school when you had to give a speech in English class and the teacher would count all your ums, ahs, and other filler words? Mine was so bad that it broke the previous record by more than triple! By this point, I had a decision to make: do I betray my intelligence by lowering my ambitions, or do I find a way to stop being so scared to speak?

I eventually left my small fishing village to go to college in a bigger city. The first year or so was rough because I did not find it easy to make friends. I never knew what to say and even when I tried, some people could not understand my mumbles. So, like most friendless losers whose intelligence and ambition outweigh their fear of ridicule, I made the obvious decision to join the debate team. I thought it would be a pretty laid back group of people who would be bound together by the mutual trauma of public speaking. At that time, the only thing I knew about debate was from a poster on campus.

I ended up joining mid-season, so everybody else seemed to already know each other. Most people in the room where the debate team practiced seemed skeptical and off-put by the stranger who trespassed into their domain. They all seemed way smarter than me, too. Clearly, I did not know what I was getting myself into.

I remember walking into the room. It immediately grew silent. Everybody stopped what they were doing and stared.

After what seemed like a really a long time of awkward silence, someone asked, "So, are you here for debate?"

I didn't know what to say. I finally said, "I guess?"

So began my competitive debate career! I was thrown into a practice round that day, even though I had never watched a debate before, and did not really keep on top of the news. The team participated in British Parliamentary debate, so the topics to be discussed and the sides the students were to defend were assigned minutes before the round began. I believe the first topic I debated had something to do with Afghanistan or General David Petraeus because I remember my partner getting chastised for making a joke, General "Betray-us," during his speech. I don't think I even knew where Afghanistan was. Or who David Petraueus was. Or why that is a distasteful joke, or why the joke would even be funny. I had deep doubts about going back. I was in way over my head.

This long-winded story is meant to illustrate why debate fosters courage. At the root of all fear is the unsettling aspect of the unknown. See, the art of debate constantly asks you to be familiar with the unknown because it will require you to answer a question you never considered before. Those questions could range from timeless philosophical enquiries to specific public policy proposals, sometimes in the same debate round. You begin to rely wholly on your own ability to problem-solve under time constraints. In many ways, your courage is what Hemingway called grace under fire, because, to do well, you are not allowed to let your inner struggles be evident in your presentation. Remember when I said travel and scholarships and groupies are on the line? You have about the same time as it takes to take a deep breath, to make multiple decisions, while a room full of smart people wait for you to make those decisions in front of their eyes. Will you perform under the pressure or will you choke?

The confidence of most debaters is shaped like an iceberg. The surface of it seems to be a colossal mass of confidence, ego, calm, and poise, but beneath that surface lays the motivation to constantly improve. That motivation is uneasiness, timidity, anxiety, self doubt. "Are these really the facts applicable to this motion? Is this the best strategy? Do I have lettuce on my teeth?" All are common questions that might come across a debater's mind before and while delivering a speech.

Apart from rising to the occasion by facing the unknown, another source of courage a debater must face is that borne of failure. In many ways, failing in front of people from whom you want respect is the best way to vanquish fear. I recall that some of my worst debate performances taught me pretty rich lessons. It is easy to feel courageous in the future when you have previously failed and realize the world did not end. There are times where you really do not know something, and it is okay to rely on others. So what, that I did not know that Omar Al-Bashir is not a nice person? Sometimes, the fear of failure is so strong in people that it prevents them from even trying.

But as you might have suspected, the more you face the unknown, and the more you lose the fear of failing, you actually start to have success. The moment when you find a cogent argument that resonates with the people you have grown to respect is something that is hard to replicate. Knowing that you have the ability to strike a chord with an audience by combining logic, reason, and emotion, you realize the power that you contain. You have the power to persuade. Persuasion means that you can change the mental identity of a person into something that you prefer in order to achieve your own goal.

These themes are fairly intertwined. As you lose the fear of the unknown, and you lose the fear of failing, and you start to become persuasive, it is partially because your analytical ability is growing. Analytical thinking is facing an unknown situation and attempting to answer it by formulating in a particular way a solution using known facts. Analytical thinking is the most difficult concept to unpack, coincidentally, because it begins to grow so gradually but so wholly that it will change the way you think forever.

To explain what analytical thinking is, I find it useful to break it down in a few stages. The first stage is to conceptualize or have a mental visual of a broad framework of the question being asked. The second stage is to formulate as many known facts as you can imagine. The third stage is to then distinguish the relevant from the irrelevant. The last and final stage is to sequence the relevant facts in order to come to a conclusion. In short, you have to prove a claim by presenting supporting evidence in a coherent manner.

In many ways, analytical thinking is very much learning through trial-and-error. Novice debaters must learn the first step and do that over and over until they can take an unknown topic and properly frame or conceptualize the question at hand. To properly answer a question, you have to understand the big picture question the asker is really aiming towards. This is the stage where the fearful student may leave debate because nothing is more frustrating than putting your entire effort into answering the wrong question and losing the debate round!

Then novice debaters must move onto formulating facts. Nothing better shows you how little you know than having to apply what you know to new questions. Here, you broaden your knowledge base by facing your own ignorance. You learn to seek out sources so that you have enough command of facts for future questions. This is where debaters begin to subscribe to *The New York Times* or *The Economist* and start finding the *New Yorker* comics funny. The last stage is one that is difficult to master, in that you have to be able to bring up the most persuasive facts in the proper sequence in order to do well in debate.

This trial-and-error type learning that occurs by debating is a lot like a blacksmith and an anvil; each round is under heated pressure and slowly your imperfections are beaten (*debatre-d*) out of you. In reality, analytical ability is a thing that has to be taught through experience. After a while, these steps automatically occur because of the "muscle memory" that develops as we test our ideas in verbal combat.

Up to this point, I have described how debate strengthens your courage by facing the unknown, coming to grips with your own lack of knowledge, and by giving you the tools to persuade others. See, this is why I think that debate, at its very core, is violent.

Debate is controversy; it is dissension; it is disrupting the social order. In order to do so, you must have the strength of your convictions. It takes ideas that may be central to the framework of society, and it prods, pokes, and pushes us to gain a better understanding of the world. Debate allows a thinker to think of how things "ought to be" or "should be" rather than stopping the thinker at "this is how it always was." Debate, therefore, is dangerous because it challenges our basic beliefs and requires evidence or reason as a basis for decision-making.

Most people in society choose to not confront others. People choose to avoid controversy because social order is an important value, and in the usual course of people's lives, outweighs being correct. In many ways, debate is offending others by merely posing questions. A posed question provides uncertainty because asking, "how should things be?" necessarily invites alternatives.

In academic debate, we attack the biggest controversies in modern societies head on. We debate topics and find points of stasis that are full of controversy. We pounce on our opponents' ideas in order to diminish their advantage. We put our own thoughts on display so they may be challenged by others. As we grow in debate, we thrive on controversy. We seek out more opportunities to embrace the controversy, grappling with big ideas so that we may test ourselves and better understand the world around us.

It is through this process that your inner personal morality will be strengthened. Most people's morals come from our experiences, but often times, they go unchallenged. This is because most people tend to live near people like themselves, and also most people find it rude to talk about religion, money, and politics with polite company. So, you would be surprised at how weak the reasons you believe the things you do, might be.

Debate helps you find your morality by exposing your beliefs to questions and evidence it never considered. At this point of my writing, you may have envisioned a person being shaped by giving lots of speeches. Truth be told, just as much learning comes from having to listen to others speak as it does actually having to speak. Your unchallenged beliefs will undoubtedly be disputed even by listening to debate rounds as you are exposed to questions and ideas that challenge your beliefs.

Suddenly, your beliefs go from being unchallenged to being posed squarely with a question, and they may even be exposed to new evidence to the contrary. Either you will answer that question (often to yourself) by finding stronger evidence, or your mind could be swayed by the strength of another's evidence. Suddenly, the things you may have lazily thought were true, you suddenly *know* are true because you weighed the evidence. Instead of basing your ideas on preconceived notions, the exposure to many different ideas now means that your ideas are based on stronger evidence.

As my debated career ended, I found myself a changed person. My personal courage had grown so much that I not only order what I want, but I will even go so far as to *ask questions about the menu* prior to ordering! That, and I applied to, got into, and attended law school. Now, I am a licensed attorney. People pay money for me to help them solve their unique problems. So my courage has definitely grown.

I also can credit my analytical abilities to debate. I often have to address unique problems, based on the fact that no two clients are the same, and no two lives are the same. So every issue I confront is something that has never been faced before. But, I take my training from law school and begin a familiar process of conceptualizing issues, brainstorming solutions, then prioritizing pieces of persuasive evidence to formulate the answers to clients' questions. I would never have gotten this far without debate.

Lastly, I can say that I can do something that I love because of debate. I found that I *always* gave my most personally impassioned speeches when I addressed law topics. Even more so, I *always* gave my most compelling arguments when specifically addressing indigenous rights, particularly in legal contexts. So, I went to law school and specialized my studies in Federal Indian law. Every day, I get to represent Native American tribal governments and craft arguments and write policies in order to help solve problems my various clients face. I do so with a lot of courage, analytical ability, and personal morality. I would not have these skills without the violent process of *debatre-ing* out my imperfections through a most violent activity by facing the unknown, by facing the fear of failure, by developing strong analytical skills, and most of all, by strengthening my inner morality. Ultimately, the most violent question a person can pose includes the words "ought" or "should."

Jonathon Sanchez grew up in a small town. He found his love for debate while attending the University of Alaska Anchorage. There, he found his passion for defending indigenous rights. He went on to graduate from the Sandra Day O'Conner College of Law at Arizona State University with an emphasis on indigenous rights. Jonathon now gets to live his life dream of advocating on behalf of Native American tribal governments at Rosette LLP, which is the preeminent firm that practices in the area of Native American rights.

From Policy Debate to Project Manager

By Ryan Davis

Dean of Business and Applied Technology

At a recent employer forum, I asked hiring managers from diverse industries about the skills and competencies needed most in their workforce. Surprisingly to some, I did not hear about coding languages, technical certifications, or college degrees; instead I heard about teamwork, critical thinking, interpreting data, and communication skills. These soft skills are increasingly part of the skills gap facing our nation's workforce. As education reformists push for sweeping changes and standardized tests that measure concrete knowledge that students can recall from the past, they are driving the curriculum away from pedagogical practices which encourage these all important skills. One answer can be found in an extracurricular activity that supports the standard curriculum and the students it serves. Policy debate alumni learn these foundation skills needed in our modern workforce, creating opportunities to meet the needs of industry and help students succeed in the modern economy.

The Critique of Policy Debate

In the debate world you often hear complaints that it is not real world enough. Policy debaters spew instead of speak, read instead of rationalize, and go wildly off topic. The lack of eloquence and persuasive speaking are instead replaced by seemingly incomprehensible delivery speeds, reliance on gigabytes of evidence, and famously dire predictions of nuclear war, ice ages, and extinction-level events. Critics would argue that students learn more applicable skills through competitions grounded in traditional podium-based speaking skills or better yet, eliminating forensic activities to meet the budget.

Let's compare debate to another popular high school academic activity: robotics. Millions of dollars have been spent building high school robotics competitions where students design, build, and demonstrate their engineering prowess. However, even with the advent of automation, few participants in these programs will go on to be robotics engineers or technicians. Instead, robotics competitions accelerate learning beyond specific technical skills. Students collaborate in teams, conduct trial and error experiments, brainstorm solutions, and research ideas. No matter if a participating student later works as an electrical engineer, registered nurse, or accountant, they apply these skills every day.

No one criticizes robotics competitions as not real world because the connection to applicable skills is much easier to visualize. While not as immediately evident to the casual observer, policy debate builds foundational skills essential in the workplace of tomorrow.

Foundational Skills for Success

In workforce development, the term soft skills refers to less tangible abilities of employees needed to function in the workplace. This term stands in contrast to hard skills such as coding languages, using specific software, or a specific license in healthcare. Hard skills land you a job, but soft skills are key to building a successful career.

So in the true spirit of policy debate, let's turn to the evidence. What are the skills employers most commonly seek in their workforce? And does policy debate enhance these skills for student participants?

The National Association of Colleges and Employers (NACE) conducted a survey in 2014 on the skills most in demand by over 250 large employers.[3] The top five most in demand abilities include: teamwork, problem solving, communication, organization, and information. (*See Table 1: Foundational Skills, located at the end of this chapter.*)

Other frameworks addressing soft skills demand include the ACT Work Readiness Standards, Global Professional Standards, and Bloomberg Skill Gap Analysis. They all reveal similar lists of in demand skills. In short, multiple analyses result in similar identifications of key soft skills for workforce success.

An analysis of employment demand adds some clarity to the picture. Using data from the Bureau of Labor Statistics Employment Projections database, I conducted an analysis of the most in demand occupations that pay a sustainable wage.[4] These occupations grouped into the following categories: licensed healthcare, software and information technology, business management, finance, and educators. Together these occupations represent nearly *40 million jobs* in the new economy, and chances are students in your classrooms today will be in one of these fields in the near future.

Table 2 takes these occupations and maps them to the list of foundational skills above by mapping it to specific skills identified in the O*NET database.[5] While it is intuitively true each of these occupations needs some level of each of the foundational skills, this method shows how critical these are for success in the modern workforce. In all five of the occupation categories listed above, three to five of the foundational skills identified by NACE are highly relevant. (*See Table 2: Occupational Categories and Foundational Skills located at the end of this chapter.*)

---

[3] For a study summary see Susan Adams, "The 10 Skills Employers Most Want In 2015 Graduates," Forbes, Nov 12, 2014,
www.forbes.com/sites/susanadams/2014/11/12/the-10-skills-employers-most-want-in-2015-graduates/#5d89623619f6 .

[4] The data table location is: http://data.bls.gov/projections/occupationProj. The filters included occupations that pay more than $50,000 annual median wages, have a total net 10 year demand of more than 10,000 projected job openings, and a growth rate of more than 10%.

[5] O*NET is a web based repository of occupational information maintained by the Department of Labor Education and Training Administration. www.onetonline.org/

Enter Policy Debate

So let's break down a policy debate round and see how debate exposes students to these key foundational skills. Though to be fair, we have to start well before the First Affirmative Constructive (1AC) to appreciate the depth and breadth of the activity.

Researching Case and Positions (Information, Organization, Teamwork)

Prior to a debate round, teams must research, write, and organize numerous positions including affirmative cases, disadvantages, counterplans, procedural arguments, critiques (or kritiks), and general evidence on the topic. First, this requires students to gather large amounts of information from a variety of sources such as academic journals, published books, and news sources. Second, this collection of information must be distilled into important evidence used to support positions on the topic. Third, debaters must create highly organized filing systems to be able to quickly locate information needed in a competitive round. Modern debate leverages technology, requiring proficiency with complex information management systems.

School teams collaborate in this process, dividing research and position development. More experienced debaters often rely on younger teams to assist with "cutting cards" and other basic research skills. Over time, skilled debaters begin crafting their own unique positions from original research and exploration.

The process of collaborative research and organization mimics requirements for many occupations. Financial analysts must gather and sift through complex financial statements and annual reports, finding key trends to share with their firm. Software development uses a team approach where senior developers lead in the algorithm process but junior developers must write the code for the product.

In-Round Strategy and Tactics (Information, Organization, and Problem Solving)

In a single debate round, a student will make dozens of decisions at both the strategic and tactical level. Prior to the start of the 1AC, teams create a preliminary approach based on their knowledge of their opponents. Once the round starts, teams create an overall strategy to win the ballot based on the information they have prepared prior to the competition. During the course of the speeches, debaters will make dozens of tactical decisions prioritizing and responding to opponents' arguments.

These decisions and the eventual outcome rely heavily on the information and organization systems brought into the round. Debaters with strong understanding of their evidence and how to locate key information are much more likely to succeed. Debaters learn in the heat of competition how information and organization are critical to quality problem solving.

The intensity and speed of a debate round translates to healthcare where physicians and nurses must make rapid decisions using multiple data sources to save patients' lives. Complex contract negotiations are won by those with superior information and the ability to choose their key issues to stand firm on.

Understanding Opponents' Arguments (Communication, Information)

Too often the benefits of debate focus on students expressing their argumentation, rather than the importance of listening and understanding. To succeed in debate, students must actively listen to opponents and understand their rhetoric. Failure to listen results in the inability to create effective counter arguments in the round.

One of the more overlooked benefits of policy debate includes exposure to views different from one's own. While annual topics drive in-depth knowledge on a particular policy issue, the breadth of argumentation is beneficial as well. In an increasingly polarized political society, students are exposed to lines of argumentation outside of their own political frame. Understanding and responding to positions using critical race theory, Marxist economic theories, or non-Americentric perspectives creates an ability to truly hear what another is saying and engage appropriately.

The vast majority of conflict in the workplace comes from a lack of understanding and communication. Healthcare professionals fail in understanding a patient's goals, teachers struggle to explain a concept in a way for a student to understand, or the unhappy worker that feels unappreciated by their manager. All of these all too real situations often result from viewing relationships and problems from a particular lens, and not being able to reach a shared understanding. Debate prepares students to uniquely address what cannot be automated: relationships between people.

As our nation's workforce becomes increasingly diverse, the ability to understand and connect with people with different cultural backgrounds is increasingly important. Debate prepares students to be able to understand diverse viewpoints and engage in constructive conversations around these differences.

Time Compression (Organization)

While the rate of speech in policy debate is often derided, the pace of the round creates intense time compression requiring highly acute organizational abilities. Managing a flow of the round and being able to respond with just seconds to think about each tactical argument simulates the often high-stress environments in today's workforce. Knowing how to quickly access evidence in your database to bring into the round saves precious seconds of prep time. In short, a debate round is ninety minutes of intense information overload.

Increasingly, businesses must be able to respond quickly to consumer demand, driven by real-time interactions through social media or web-based platforms. Agile projects require rapid reaction and innovation, bringing innovative technologies to market implementation using iterative and interactive processes. In short, the flow of information available continues to accelerate, and the ability to function in an information-saturated environment is increasingly critical.

Winning Your Argument (Problem Solving, Teamwork, Communication, Organization, Information)

Executing winning argumentation in a debate round requires debaters to demonstrate all of the foundational skills. Below are some common ways that teams win rounds and the competencies that must be demonstrated to win a ballot:

Superior Evidence (Information, Organization, Communication): Possessing case turns, recent uniqueness cards, and specific kritik answers create an immediate advantage in the round. This requires extensive research before the round, and the organizational and communicative ability to quickly bring the evidence onto the flow at the right time.

Better Reasoning (Problem Solving, Communication): While policy debate tends to be evidence heavy, many rounds can be won on better reasoning alone. Counterplans with incredible solvency cannot withstand a clever permutation and even the best-evidenced teams can fall into a double turn trap. With dozens of individual arguments and cards on the flow, finding winning opportunities requires complex problem-solving capacity and the ability to articulate your reasoning to the judge.

Forcing Dropped Arguments (Communication, Organization): Just like in college football where there can be great mismatches between teams, some debate rounds come down to just better skills. Novice and junior teams can often be overwhelmed by the information overload presented by a faster speaking or more experienced team. That is, they find themselves spread out of a round by an experienced duo, simply because they are unable to keep up with the pace of the round.

Even in closer matched rounds, overwhelming the 1AR with depth or breadth can result in easy wins. However, being able to spread your opponent too thin requires not just the ability to speak quickly, but requires effective organization to bring the right evidence to bear in the round.

Better Collapse Strategy (Problem Solving, Teamwork): Better-prepared and better tactical debate teams often falter because of poor strategy in final rebuttals. Being able to identify the best arguments requires close collaboration between team members. In the negative block, the division of arguments and a preliminary strategy put pressure on the 1AR and allow for a clear reason for decision.

On the affirmative side, teams must collaborate to make sure the 1AR picks the arguments critical to the closing speech. Making the right choices as the debate distills into rebuttals requires the ability to evaluate and process multiple potential outcomes and then execute the correct strategy.

Conclusion: Hire Former Debaters

Few jobs require the ability to speak 300 words per minute or debate the next threat of nuclear Armageddon. However, in-demand jobs in the modern economy demand exceptional capacity to problem-solve, communicate with diverse audiences, manage large quantities of information, work with cross-functional teams, and function in fast-paced environments. Many extra-curricular activities can build these skills, allowing students to build competencies in simulated environments. Policy debate may not have the trendy appeal of robotics or the fan base of football. Nevertheless, debaters learn and practice critical skills that will serve them for decades after their last rebuttal.

Ryan Davis serves as Dean of Business and Applied Technology at Everett Community College in Washington State and the President of the Washington State Workforce Education Council. He is a graduate of the United States Air Force Academy and completed his Masters in Public Administration at the University of Washington Evans School of Public Policy and Governance. Ryan has led major workforce initiatives funded by the Department of Labor, Commerce, Energy, and Transportation throughout the Pacific Northwest. Additionally, he serves as a board member for Workforce Snohomish, TechWorks, and Infralign social ventures.

Table 1: Foundational Skills

Rank	Foundational Skill	Definition
1	Teamwork	The ability to work in a team structure both as a leader and team member.
2	Problem Solving	The ability to diagnose, solve, and make decisions to resolve complex issues.
3	Communication	The ability to communicate verbally with people inside and outside an organization.
4	Organization	The ability to plan, organize, and prioritize work in time constrained environments.
5	Information	The ability to obtain, organize, and process information from multiple sources.

Table 2: Occupational Categories and Foundational Skills

Category	Example Occupations	Teamwork	Problem Solving	Communication	Organization	Information
Licensed Healthcare	Registered Nurse, Physician Assistant, Physical Therapist		Yes	Yes	Yes	Yes
Software and Information Technology	Software Developer, Systems Admin, Information Security	Yes	Yes		Yes	Yes
Business Management	Operations Manager, District Manager, Management Consultant	Yes		Yes	Yes	Yes
Finance	Certified Public Accountant, Financial Planner, Comptroller		Yes		Yes	Yes
Educators	Elementary Teacher, College Instructor, Corporate Trainer	Yes		Yes	Yes	

Why We Debate: A Corporate Leadership Perspective

By Luke Savoie

General Manager and Vice President of L-3 ForceX

As a senior executive, debate has played a major role in shaping my ability to do my job today. Enabling me with critical skills, debate has been instrumental to overcoming challenges on my path to the boardroom. Currently, I am a Vice President with L-3 Communications and the General Manager of their ForceX division in Nashville, Tennessee. I came to know the lead author of this book as a freshman in college, and it was he who introduced me to competitive debate.

Growing up in an extremely loud and passionate Italian family, I was no stranger to the art of argument. More importantly, debate started me down a path of listening to what was being said in a room and formulating what I was going to say. Most importantly when you spoke, you could guarantee there would be a response and multiple counterarguments, so I learned to be on the offensive and ensure any initial action on my part would already contain key elements to disarm the first volley of retorts from my opponents: Mom, Dad, aunts, and uncles. College debate honed those skills in a four year pressure cooker that formalized the process and provided further and further confidence to speak in any situation. This has direct application to my work today.

L-3, being a large publicly traded company, requires continual engagement at higher echelons. This engagement is where we typically determine the strategy for long-term objectives and crisis management of short-term issues. *Critical problem-solving skills, making-data driven decisions, and being able to communicate objectives are key.* In policy debate, research is necessary to make every argument; evidence must be presented, sources vetted, and key components of the evidence brought to the forefront.

Debate has enabled me to read volumes of financial data, new business opportunities, or diligence reports for a new acquisition, and condense what the evidence is saying into concise portions that can be presented to the various decision-makers at my company. Many in the boardroom call these the takeaways, and in policy debate we called them the tags.

In 1997, Shawn and I perfected the art of the tag with the affirmative cases we wrote for the Cross Examination Debate Association season. We had multiple affirmative cases that dealt with Proliferation of Nuclear Weapons, Biotechnology, and Trans-National Criminal Organizations, to name just a few. Most of our first affirmative constructives (1ACs)—the introduction to the debate—contained more than *thirty* pieces of evidence, or cards.

Researching volumes of evidence was required to make those cases that year; more importantly condensing the evidence down and providing the best tags for each card was needed to even read all of it in the allotted amount of time.

In the boardroom the same applies. I often have to present complex financial data or technical solutions we are pitching, in ways that are easily understood by other members of our organization or potential customers. Being able to condense the information into critical takeaways is needed to get people who are extremely time-constrained to understand your position and approve your strategy.

Out of the boardroom and in dealing with my customers, debate taught me *how to preempt my competitors' arguments.* Often, I know who has been to a customer location and what their angle is to providing solutions for a particular client. Debate taught me to incorporate within my pitch the first round of counterarguments. It also taught me to continually tailor those counterarguments based upon which competitors I know were there.

For instance, in the 1996-1997 season of debate, we knew that certain schools were always going to attack our case on topicality, an argument which states that we had exceeded the parameters established for the debate by the resolution. So when we debated those schools, we would cut out one of the doomsday scenarios that justified our policy proposal and replace it with a three-card argument at the end of the 1AC, framing the debate purely on the merits of the policy versus the arbitrary and vague boundaries established by a stock issue like topicality.

When making a brief, white paper, or a proposal for a customer, I naturally ensure that there are focused counterpoints to my competitors' pitches. This approach has been very effective for my company. Nevertheless, I took this too far once with a customer. A new boss had been hired to run the division of this particular customer, and I was required to go brief him with a team of folks from my company. I discovered that a competitor had already met with this customer and planted multiple landmines (figuratively) with the new executive, to purposely undermine our business with them. When I started the brief the following day, I immediately got asked a question and I knew exactly where it was coming from. I proceeded to disarm the argument. In my following slides, I preempted the questions I knew were coming, with counterarguments along the way. This was necessary, but unfortunately I went over on time, and the end portion of the brief (where my boss got to speak) was skipped. Suffice to say, she was not entirely thrilled.

Along these same lines, debate also taught me *how to steer the conversation a certain way.* Like the example above, we always attempted to strike first and frame how the round would be judged. Often in business, I try to get customers to frame their decision-calculus around capabilities that I know my company excels at, and which play to the true needs of the customer.

Debate continually taught me to *weigh the disposition of the judge* and ensure that I either brought the judge over to our way of thinking or adapted to the judge if they were immoveable. I mentor my business development managers in this even today to do their competitive research, understand their audience and how the competitors will approach that same audience, how to strike first, and how to frame the decision based on our company's strengths.

Debate made me *think not only on my feet, but also made me think more quickly.* Policy debate in college is extremely fast paced. Reading dozens of cards or ripping off multiple counterarguments is par for the course in policy. I was notorious in college, especially as the first negative constructive for spreading the opposing team out of the debate by essentially developing more arguments in my first speech than they could respond to in their subsequent speech. Although being able to talk extremely fast was helpful, that was not really the name of the game. There was actually much more going on than most outsiders recognize.

On the affirmative, I was also the first speaker and had the difficult task of delivering an effective first affirmative rebuttal (1AR). The 1AR is by far the toughest speech in a policy debate round because the speaker has five minutes to respond to thirteen minutes of negative argumentation. This forces the debater to move through the positions with speed and precision. In this way, I honed my ability to listen strategically, develop the most important responses, and precisely leverage those ideas against my opponent's arguments. This aspect of policy debate aided my ability to take notes (flow) and respond to a host of arguments in a short amount of time extremely quickly, faster than most in my peer group in industry.

The ability to listen, write down the arguments of those in my boardroom, align all the arguments and counterarguments, and determine the gaps has been a key element to operating effectively in business. I learned all of that directly from my time in college policy debate where debaters developed multiple lines of argument while simultaneously speaking in the neighborhood of 350-450 words per minute, nearly five times normal conversational pace.

Finally, *the construction of a plan was probably the most impactful* thing from debate that I learned and use in everyday life at work. In policy debate, assessing the need (as determined by the resolution), determining a focused thing to do about it, constructing the details of what to do, and assessing the impacts of it (or impacts that it prevents) were a lesson I learned in policy debate.

This became the foundation of what attracted me to Systems Engineering, which became the foundation of the solutions my company provides. Assessing the core need or mission of the customer, determining the critical capabilities gaps, and providing focused solutions to those gaps is the essence of what we do. In my business, instead of impacts of inaction that a normal affirmative would argue or impacts of action that the negative would argue, we have risks. Determining program risks and outlining them (technical, cost, schedule) is a basic element of how we tackle each and every project we do. Doing risk assessment is a basic element in debate. What is the risk of doing this plan, what is the risk of not? In policy debate we usually evaluate this through the lives lost or saved as a result of enacting a plan.

In my business, the same applies (via airworthiness or weapons programs) but mostly is about mission effectiveness, cost control, and schedule control. In my business, these aspects of plan construction are how I mentor all my program managers and systems engineers. We call it a BLUF (Bottom Line Up Front). What is the focused thing we are solving for the customer? Tell the customer the solution based on the premise in the BLUF. Provide an assessment of risks for this approach and usually demonstrate how it is less risky than our competitors' methods. The way a plan or counterplan is formulated is exactly how we do this each day with the approach of our solutions; the main difference is that instead of having one resolution for the whole year, each customer has a unique challenge that is the resolution and the BLUF is our plan text.

Debate was an extremely rewarding time for me when I was in school. The hours spent in preparation for a season, the continual improvement of our arguments and evidence over the course of the year, and the back and forth that occurred in debate rounds are things that will stay with me forever.

On reflection, of all my studies, debate played the most significant role in preparing me for life outside of school. It enabled me to be successful in pilot training, on the battlefield, back in school doing post-graduate work at Johns Hopkins University, and in business. I have never had any trouble with public speaking nor have I ever been apprehensive to take questions from people in any setting. Debate helped me think on my feet and doing it competitively is what made it instinctual. I can think of no academic endeavor that could prepare an individual more than debate, in any of its forms or formats.

Luke Savoie is a Vice President with L-3 Communications and the General Manager of its ForceX Division within Electronic Systems Group. Prior to joining L-3 ForceX, he was an instructor pilot in the U.S. Air Force where he served for 10 years, mostly in Air Force Special Operations Command. He has over 2,000 combat hours of flight experience in the AC-130U gunship as an Aircraft Commander and as an Instructor Pilot in the U-28As. He graduated from the United States Air Force Academy with a Bachelor of Science in General Sciences and a minor in Philosophy and earned his Executive Master of Business Administration from the Johns Hopkins Carey Business School.

Leading Nonprofit Organizations

By Amy Cram Helwich

Executive Director of the Minnesota Urban Debate League

I joined the Cheyenne East High School debate team when I was 15 years old, and my life was changed. Many folks can document how debate was a transformative experience for themselves personally, but few also have the great pleasure of continuing in debate as a professional. I am one of the lucky few, having returned to the world of debate to run the Minnesota Urban Debate League in 2009.

Prior to joining the debate team I was quiet, shy, and some-what awkward. I loved politics though. I spent hours talking about the Iran Contra affair at the dinner table with my dad. I was passionate about social justice, though I didn't quite have that frame of reference yet. And, I was an unapologetic feminist. Debate gave me the space to test out my ideas, develop strong friendships, and most importantly, help me build my self-confidence.

Debate continued to be transformative-as I went on to Casper College and then the University of Wyoming on debate scholarships, met my future husband at a debate tournament, and watched happily as my younger siblings also excelled in the activity. My senior year of college I had a momentary career planning panic. I decided I really didn't want to go to law school after all, unlike many of my debate teammates and competitors. I enjoyed learning about policy issues, and I also wanted to make a meaningful contribution to the wider world. After a series of conversations with my political science advisor and cramming for the GRE, I was accepted on a full scholarship by the University of Pittsburgh's Graduate School for Public and International Affairs to enroll in its Master of Public Administration (MPA) program.

Without a doubt, my high school and college debate experiences prepared me for a rigorous graduate school experience and laid the groundwork for my future career. In reflecting back on my career and leadership positions, I would say that my debate training was particularly useful in three different areas:

1. Public Speaking and Self-Confidence

2. Research and Grant Writing

3. Fundraising and Leadership

Public Speaking and Self-Confidence

Starting graduate school was a significant time of both personal and academic growth. I was newly married, had moved across the country to live in an exciting urban area, and embarked on a competitive master's degree program. As I started graduate school, I wondered if I was academically prepared; coming from a community college and then a small state school, self-doubt was not far behind. The confidence that participating in debate brings was a lifeline in this time of transition.

One of my first major research assignments was to examine a compelling policy issue, discuss the causes and possible solutions, and then be prepared to give a timed speech about the paper; essentially everything I had learned in debate since I was 15 years old.

While my experience in policy debate in the 1990s was less focused on rhetoric, and more focused on critical thinking and speed reading, I also learned how to adapt to a variety of different audiences and judges. My coaches had always been clear that it was my responsibility to adapt to my audience. In fact, I still hear my college coach invoking the "adapt or die" motto. Through that process of learning to speak to the judge at the back of the room, I also learned important elements of public speaking: standing up straight, projecting my voice, vocal inflection, making eye contact, and connecting with the audience.

The need to continue to adapt to my audience in my professional life is real. As the director of a nonprofit, I am regularly called upon to address a wide array of potential audiences, both small and large. Prior to any speech or important meeting, I begin by first conducting an audience analysis. What is their interest? Where does my interest align with theirs? How can I persuade them, and what evidence is needed to make my case? This remains true whether I am speaking with school district officials, potential donors, or foundation representatives.

While I still get nervous when giving major public speeches (as most people do), I am forever grateful that I started learning how to do this well at a young age. To try and fail, but also sometimes succeed, in competitive debate made me dramatically more prepared in graduate school and my first job, than if I had to learn public speaking early in my career. A high school debater who has attended four weekend tournaments over the course of the year, along with four months of practices, can easily attain eighty hours of program time. Take this amount of time, multiply it across years and you will find an alumni core of students who can articulate the complexities of substantial policy issues while persuading you of their choice of action. I am so glad I am an alumna.

Research and Grant Writing

One of the greatest skills I learned through debate was how to research effectively and read articles for evidence. When I started debate, access to computer search engines was just becoming available, and a road trip to the University of Colorado for access to Lexus Nexus provided fun team-building opportunities. Debate introduced me to the power of electronic search engines and how to use them effectively. With incredible ease of access to information at their fingertips, debate students now have a very different challenge: how to sift through the wealth of resources available on the Internet, locate the best evidence, and also determine the quality of evidence.

Effective research and the ability to outline my argument, bolstered by evidence, were the cornerstones to my first professional job: grant writing. While completing my MPA degree, I also participated in a fellowship for Grantmakers of Western Pennsylvania, a membership organization for foundations. I learned about foundations, philanthropy, and the process to solicit grants for funding. Shortly after I graduated, I began my career by coordinating a capital campaign for a YMCA southwest of Pittsburgh with a goal of raising $2.5 million.

I learned an extraordinary amount in this first job. I was responsible for coordinating and planning events, making in-person calls in partnership with the organization's board members for gifts, and developing a grant calendar and plan for submission of grants.

While I was learning on the job, debate certainly helped prepare me and gave me a professional advantage. I found that writing a grant was very similar to writing an affirmative case. Core sections of a grant application often ask to detail what the problem or challenge may be, how that problem came into existence, what your plan of action will be to address the challenge, how you know your program will be successful in meeting that challenge, and what outcomes or advantages might be created based on the successful program.

Whether I was writing a grant for the Mon Valley YMCA, Big Brothers Big Sisters of the Greater Twin Cities, or the Minnesota Urban Debate League, the core fundamentals of outlining my argument, making choices on the best evidence to support my argument, and showcasing the passion for my particular program were all a part of a winning proposal.

Perhaps this was most true when I applied for-and won-three federal grant competitions. (Department of Education once, and Department of Justice twice). National, state, or large competitive grant programs, such as the United Way, often have an intense and specific grant application process. To create a winning proposal, it is critical to analyze sections thoroughly to determine what they are looking for, as each section is scored separately. Since grant applications usually have strict limits on the number of pages or characters that may be used in the grant application, it is imperative to make sound choices in determining which of their goals should be targeted, and which aspects of a program will demonstrate key connections (or internal links) to them. Finally, I must be able to self-reflect and determine how effectively I answered the question posed in the grant application. The ability to develop those cases (or arguments) and analyze the linkages within them is definitely something I learned from debate.

Fundraising and Leadership

After my first job with the Mon Valley YMCA, my husband and I moved to the Twin Cities, Minnesota, in 2002. My career in the Twin Cities began with me working as a grant manager and then director of foundation and corporate relations for Big Brothers Big Sisters. After almost three years, I went on to become the director of development at small organizations: Growth and Justice, and then Children's Safety Centers. In 2007, I had significant career growth when I became the development director of the Women's Foundation of Minnesota, a state-wide community foundation.

At the age of 29, I found myself helping lead a $15 million comprehensive endowment campaign and managing a team of five. I was incredibly excited about this opportunity to fundraise for a social justice mission, to help eradicate systemic oppression, and to take on one of my most significant professional challenges to date.

I had moments of great doubt regarding whether I was up to the task or fully prepared. But once again, I was able to rely on my early debate skills to help build my confidence in taking on this challenge.

In this new role, I was analyzing reports to determine donor patterns and analytics. I was writing annual appeal letters and creating cultivation strategies. I was also learning how to be an effective manager and support my team.

Fundraising at its core is about persuasion. Can you persuade someone that a cause is important? Can you persuade them that it is important enough that they should donate their time, talent, or treasure? And can you do this with so many other demands for their attention in the nonprofit marketplace?

Debate gave me a set of transferable skills to the fundraising profession. Critical thinking skills that helped me develop a data-based approach to analyzing donor benchmarks. Argument construction, with a focus on evidence, to move donors who are very focused on outcomes, is incredibly important. In fact, it becomes more important every year in this sector. And passion-not being afraid of pathos for an emotional appeal of reaching donor's hearts as well as their minds-to discover the magic and joy of this work.

My last career jump was in 2009, when I became the Executive Director of the Minnesota Urban Debate League. This undertaking was a true joy and an incredible professional challenge, as we grew from serving 150 students at fifteen schools to almost 750 students at thirty-eight schools today. I am grateful for the opportunity to give back to an activity that was transformative for me in so many ways. I am also grateful for all that I have learned from others in the activity-colleagues, teachers, coaches, and students.

In addition to all the other debate skills that I have applied to my professional career, perhaps one of the most important in being a fundraiser is emotional resilience. Just like in debate, when you lose before you win, in fundraising you must have thick skin and the ability to bounce back. You will be told "no" to a funding request many more times than "yes." It will be hard. But you will dust yourself off and get back into the game. You will listen when a funder gives you constructive feedback (just as judges did), and you will learn what you can do better the second or third time around. And you will persist and excel.

When I thought of what my career might be in college, I had no idea what being a fundraiser or working in philanthropy could possibly entail. I am glad and grateful that I found my way into this rewarding work, and I would encourage more debaters to enter the field.

Amy Cram Helwich is the Executive Director of the Minnesota Urban Debate League, a program of Augsburg College. She holds a Masters of Public Administration from the University of Pittsburgh, and a Bachelor of Science in Political Science from the University of Wyoming. Amy has over 15 years of nonprofit management experience and believes in debate as a transformative activity for educational access. Amy is also married, has two children, and lives in St. Paul, MN.

Off We Go

By Lt. Col. Dave Haworth

Pilot in the U.S. Air Force

On the evening of 23 September 2014, I was sitting in the conference room of the Combined Air Operations Center in Doha, Qatar. It is a massive building that looks like it is sinking into the sand that surrounds it. By the time you make it past the three security checkpoints and into the operations center, you quickly forget you are in the Middle East. Instead, you feel like you are on a movie set with five massive 40-foot by 40-foot screens with radar tracks and videos from unmanned airplanes. As the Director of Combat Operations, I was responsible for every military airplane that flew in the twenty-nation theater.

That night, however, my focus was on Syria. An international coalition was about to penetrate Syrian regime air defenses and strike ISIL targets in that country for the very first time. The strike was divided into three parts: first, over fifty Tomahawk cruise missiles from ships in the Arabian Gulf; second, a U.S. strike package, including the very first combat mission of the F-22 Raptor; third, an international package consisting of aircraft from seven countries. As I finished the go/no-go brief to Lieutenant General John Hesterman and he relayed that message back to General Lloyd Austin at United States Central Command, I paused for just a second, maybe less, and thought: "How did I get here?"

For me, I think the single event, or collection of events, that put me in the chair that night was debate. I remember the very first meeting for those interested in joining the debate team. My dad had been a debater in college. He would talk about his friends and some of the trips as I was growing up, but we never really talked about the debates themselves. Maybe I was curious, or maybe it was a chance to find some friends and go on some trips like my dad. Whatever it was I was hooked from the very first meeting.

The West Orange-Stark Speech and Debate team had a good coach and some talent. As I started to learn about the events, I gravitated more towards policy debate rather than the individual speech events. Our coach made all the debaters compete in the individual events. He would lecture us on being well rounded, or something like that. At the time, I suspected it was just to get more points for the overall team awards. I always considered it a waste of time; after all *I could be prepping for the next round!* Today, I am sure there were skills developed in some of those impromptu or extemporaneous events, but I drew the line at prose and poetry readings.

I was anxious to get to my first tournament. I was so excited to earn points for the National Forensic League (NFL) awards. I have no idea if the ruby, quadruple ruby, or diamond awards still exist, or if the NFL even exists today, but that was such an important part of my high school experience. (I've since discovered that the NFL still recognizes students, although it is now known as the National Speech & Debate Association.) I have no idea why they were important; they were just little stickers that I put onto the certificate. There was just something about points, awards, and wins that appealed to me. Nevertheless, the competitive aspect of debate was very important to me, and I think debate provides an outlet for that academic *competition* like no other activity.

As I progressed in the Air Force, competition was a critical part of development. The path to becoming a fighter pilot is competitive, but the lifestyle of a fighter pilot is constant competition. Every task, every flight, every weapon released, whether simulated or delivered in combat, is planned, executed, and then graded or debriefed. Results are posted and everyone in the unit knows their standing in the pecking order of a fighter squadron every day. I learned about the concept of very public rankings at debate tournaments early on when results are posted, elimination rounds are announced, awards are presented, and when you read ballots on the way home.

After attending my first few tournaments, I realized I did not want to merely watch others win trophies; I wanted to win, and I wanted my teammates to win. If I hoped to achieve any level of success during the tournaments, then I had to devote time in *preparation* for the activity. Research is the foundation for a policy team.

Our squad filled cases and cases with research. Rolling the dolly of tubs into a tournament was an act of intimidation as much as anything else. I always suspected some teams wheeled tubs filled with blank pages just for show. When the real competition began, however, those teams quickly disappeared. They might win a round or two on skill or charm, but without the evidence, eventually an argument falls apart.

That was another great lesson for me: do your homework. The unique part of debate preparation is the research that is conducted on both sides of the argument. That is a life skill that few people fully appreciate. The ability to think and reason for the other side of a point helps to win an argument, and I also think it helps to develop a broader understanding of topics. During my time in debate, I learned that putting in the time, paying attention to the details, and thinking through the material matter.

My early lessons on preparation helped me achieve and succeed at a dream come true—my selection as an Air Force Thunderbird. For two years I served as the Thunderbird Advance Pilot and Narrator. I cannot imagine a more fitting example of preparation than the world's greatest aerial demonstration team. Flying a few feet away from another F-16 at 500 miles per hour in close proximity to the ground is not a task to be taken lightly. It is also not a task to be done quickly. Every year from December until March the team flies multiple sorties, or missions, per day at wide distances and higher altitudes until maneuvers are perfected. Only then do you move closer and lower, until eventually it becomes second nature. That process and preparation permeates every aspect of the team. Everything the Thunderbirds do—from how to polish boots to how to conduct an inverted pass—is planned, executed, and debriefed to perfection.

All that preparation, however, means little if you cannot convey your ideas clearly to others. As the narrator for the Thunderbirds I was responsible for translating the fighter pilots' language into one the seven million spectators a year we would perform in front of could understand. The same was true in debate. I needed to translate the tubs of research into something that would convince a judge to vote for my team. I learned a variety of *communication* styles while I was debating. For a period, the more you said the better, so speed was the name of the game. The policy rounds in my day featured a cross-examination period where I learned to develop my questioning skills. Whatever styles or techniques developed over time, I believe the most important aspect of debate was just the ability to feel comfortable speaking in front of large and small audiences. That might not sound like much, but I cannot count the number of times I have seen exceptionally talented men and women fail because of the inability to speak in public.

It was this comfort speaking to both small and large audiences that created some incredible opportunities during my career. I have narrated A-10 demonstration teams as well as the Thunderbirds. I have done more television and newspaper interviews than I can count, including a CBS *60 Minutes* segment. I narrated the opening of the Air Force Memorial in Washington, D.C. For each of those events, it was the ability to give an in-class presentation in college, or a no-notice briefing at work, or a VIP tour to high ranking officials that paved the way for whatever success I have enjoyed, and I owe *all* of that to the very basic skills developed in debate. That is the life-long gift the activity can give to anyone that chooses to participate at whatever level.

While learning a life-long skill is noble, as I said before, debate for me was about winning. Unfortunately, there were many rounds, especially in my early debating years, where I knew my team had the better research and we were the better communicators, but we still lost the round. How could the soccer mom, gym coach, or bus driver judge not see the dropped topicality argument or the case turn on the disad? The judges did not see those topics or issues and ended up voting against me because *they had no idea what I was talking about!* What I finally learned was that while I may have been debating the other team, I was actually trying to convince the one person in the room with a ballot to vote for us. It did not matter if my opponent understood my efforts, if I did not clearly communicate with the judge in a language he or she understood. I never had a term for the concept when I was debating, but I think researchers today would likely call it *emotional intelligence.* The ability to recognize someone else's emotions, reactions, and feelings.

That is a skill that everyone uses every day. After all, I do not need to fight my point with a sibling or colleague; I just need my parent or boss to agree with me. Nowhere was this lesson more telling than my assignment to the Pentagon. I simply could not understand how colleagues of mine could not recognize the importance of communicating with key leaders around Washington, D.C. Discussions with young congressional staffers or White House members with little or no military experience were critical to future budgets and acquisition matters. Now I would never compare a congressional staffer to an uneducated debate judge, but the ability to understand their processing capacity for complex military information was critical if we were presenting an important position. In those instances losing the round, but consoling each other with the idea that the staffer just did not understand would be potentially disastrous for the Air Force. So unless someone is planning on being isolated on a desert island, understanding how to relate to people is another important skill to learn.

That is not to say that manipulating people is the goal of a debate competition. The real goal is an academically challenging competition on important issues of the time. At the end of the day, however, win or lose, the most important part for me was the people. I always enjoyed the *team* aspect of debate immensely. I experienced the activity on both large and small programs. In both extremes, the ability to understand each other's strengths and talents was critical to the overall team and individual success. Pairing the right talents into an individual team was also important. In high school, I was mostly a first speaker and then switched in college to being mostly a 2. Both positions required different skill sets and I was lucky to find partners during high school and college that complemented me and vice versa. We spent lots of time together, we had great times, and we had massive fights, but at the end of the day we were always partners. I have an older brother, a younger sister, and had girlfriends in high school and college, but my debate partners taught me more about true partnership than anyone else in my life, up until I got married.

The concept of team and partner is something I think people are always searching for. That professional relationship in a fighter squadron is a wingman. Without making any *Top Gun* jokes, the wingman is the person that has your back, who you trust with your life. In multiple combat tours I have had wingmen literally save my life. The very foundations of true trust and partnership for those life-saving skills I can trace all the way back to the debate team at West Orange.

Overall, there is not a day that goes by that I do not think about debate or use the skills I developed over the eight years I participated in the activity. I was able to achieve some great recognition while I was competing. I was a two-time state champion in high school and earned an All-American award my senior year at the U.S. Air Force Academy. After graduation, I went on to fly A-10s and F-16s in the Air Force, including a tour with the Thunderbirds. And on one night in 2014 I gave the order: "launch the TLAMS, the strike's a go." Not bad for a small town Texas kid, and it all started 28 years ago when I walked in a room and asked, "Is this the meeting about the debate team?"

So why should you debate? I think it teaches great lessons in competition, preparation, communication, emotional intelligence, and teamwork. Is that why I did it? No, not really. I debated for eight years because it was fun. I made some great friends and took some really cool trips, and those are the stories I tell my son.

Dave Haworth entered the United States Air Force in 1995 after graduating from the United States Air Force Academy. He attended flight training and was selected to fly fighter aircraft. Lt. Col. Haworth is an instructor pilot in A-10s and F-16s, and has accumulated over 3,000 hours of flight time. In 2003, then-Captain Haworth was selected for the Air Force Thunderbirds, and served two years as the Advance Pilot and Narrator. Lt. Col. Haworth has multiple combat deployments in Kosovo and Afghanistan. His awards include the Distinguished Flying Cross and fourteen Air Medals.

Engineering Discourse

By Marshall McMullen

Principal Engineer at NetApp SolidFire

I started debate at an early age in middle school as part of a gifted education program where I was introduced to the basics of policy debate. In high school, debate became an all-consuming passion that I spent every waking minute thinking about in some way. While I intended to continue with policy debate in high school, our small town program did not have enough people to form another policy debate team, so I ended up in Lincoln-Douglas (LD) debate. As it turns out, this was a great fit as I had an intense passion for philosophy and learning to critically analyze and argue about unquantifiable and polarizing ideas.

I continued this passion in college at the United States Air Force Academy where I returned to policy debate as a four-year competitor in the Cross Examination Debate Association. After graduation, I had every intention of attending law school and furthering the skillsets and experience I had spent ten years developing. But life had other plans for me.

I am currently a Principal Engineer for NetApp SolidFire, and thoroughly enjoy software development as intensely as I did debate. While this seems like an unlikely fit for someone with a background in debate, philosophy, and pre-law, I strongly believe that my experience in debate has a direct correlation on my success as a software engineer.

During the last fifteen years I have transformed myself into an extremely technical software developer. I went back to college at the University of Arizona and took all the classes normally offered in a typical Bachelor of Science degree in Computer Science. I enjoyed the material so much that I continued on to acquire my Master's Degree in Computer Science. In the years that followed, I accepted an extremely challenging role as a Kernel Developer for IBM. I climbed the proverbial corporate and technical ladders through various employers, obtaining extensive knowledge and experience culminating in my current position as Principal Software Engineer. Obviously, I had to acquire extensive technical knowledge to reach my current position. However, that technical knowledge was *necessary* but not *sufficient* for success. Surprising as it may sound, there are a lot of parallels between the world of computer programming and academic debate. The many lessons and skills I learned in debate turned out to be the linchpin in my success as a software engineer.

Research

One of the most tangible and practical skills debate imparts is the ability to conduct effective research. Consider the parallels between a debater researching a new topic and a software engineer implementing some form of new technology. When debaters receive a new topic they feverishly research every aspect of the topic to look for ideas for cases, counterplans, advantages, and disadvantages. Software developers go through a very similar process when researching new technology. They perform extensive research into the technology to understand all aspects of it including its tradeoffs, strengths, weaknesses, and limitations. In both these scenarios the research being performed is of a very exploratory nature. This means that both debaters and software developers are not researching something specific at this point, but are doing very general research to learn about the topic or technology. This type of exploratory research requires someone capable of synthesizing a large amount of seemingly disjointed and unrelated information and distill it down into something simple, logical, and cohesive.

Another interesting parallel exists between debaters researching a particular debate argument and trying to find its flaws and software developers researching why a bug in their software exists. Debaters research all aspects of an argument to uncover its assumptions, biases, and logical fallacies in order to mount an attack against the argument or be better prepared to defend against it. When a software developer works on a bug they often scour the Internet looking for similar bug reports.

Debaters often read the original source of an argument in order to better understand the author's perspective. Similarly, software developers often read the original source code of a program in order to gain more insight into the internal workings of the program.

Debaters often talk through issues with their teammates in order to better understand the position at a theoretical level and better explain the position when in a round of competition. Similarly, software developers often brainstorm and whiteboard a problem with one another to try to figure out the problem and find the best possible solution. Researching a bug often requires combing through heaps of output from a program to ascertain what the software did.

Debaters often read vigorously on current social and political issues to see how they might apply to their current topic or various disadvantages they are writing. This is very similar to software developers who need to stay current on technological trends and new developments to see how the new technology may apply to features they are working on or future developments on the roadmap.

Debaters are required to process and aggregate massive amounts of information and synthesize that evidence into something useful which can be applied to their current topic. Similarly, software developers have to stay on top of a rapidly developing technological landscape. The sheer magnitude and speed at which this field continually evolves makes this problem extremely challenging to wrangle. Software developers often solve this sort of problem with RSS (Rich Site Summary) news feeds based on particular keywords much like debaters historically used tools such as Lexus-Nexus to monitor and research a topic.

Analysis

The parallels between debate and software development run a lot deeper than the mere mechanics of research. There is an extensive amount of analysis that goes on behind the scenes in these two fields that draw from very similar skill sets. Ultimately, both debate and software development hinge on the ability to take a large complex issue and break it down into its component pieces and understand how they relate to one another. Let's look at the analytical skills both fields require in more depth.

Consider a typical disadvantage in debate. A disadvantage can typically be broken down into component pieces such as uniqueness, link, internal links, and impact. A debater must then analyze each of these component pieces as they fit into the larger story of the disadvantage for consistency. Then the debater examines each of these components individually to see if they fulfill their requirements. From there the debater examines the internal linkage within the argument to see if the argument makes logical sense and is backed up by sound evidence.

Consider then what a software developer goes through while debugging a problem in their code. They start by examining the bug report and ensuring they understand at a high level what is expected from the software and how it is failing to meet that expectation. The software developer then typically looks through the logs from the software to understand what the software did. This is similar in purpose to reading evidence to see if it backs up an argument. A deeper analysis is often required by consulting the source code directly and tracing through what the code purports to perform. An interesting analogy here would be to think of the log files from the software as quotes or excerpts from an argument whereas the source code is closer to the original author's argument. Both are required to make sense of what the program is supposed to do versus what it is actually doing.

Critically analyzing a position in debate involves breaking the position down into its component pieces and figuring out how they relate to one another in the same way that a systems programmer logically dissects a program down into modular pieces for easier comprehension and debugging.

Just as important as deconstruction is the ability to synthesize component pieces and see how they interact within a larger system. The best debaters are generally not the ones that win every single response on the line-by-line debate but the ones who can synthesize all the many arguments in a debate round into something cohesive. This same thing is true of adept software developers. The most talented software developers are the ones that can look past the individual components and strive to understand how they interact as a larger system. This allows them to think ahead of where the software needs to be in future releases as new features and products come down the pipeline.

Software Design Process

The software design process is a manifestation of debate in numerous ways. There are many different software design processes used throughout the software industry (e.g. Waterfall Development, Agile Development, etc.) but all of them share a common thread in that they have some sort of discrete design phase. There are many profound similarities between the software design process and the structure of a debate round and its imperative towards decision-making.

During the design phase of software development, software developers create a feature specification document that includes several elements with direct debate parallels. While the exact content of a feature specification can vary significantly from one development team to another, they generally include the following key sections. First, there is the purpose section of the document, wherein the objective of the overall feature is explained and a clear delineation is made between what the feature is and what it is not.

This is similar to a debate topic, which is often a very broad subject that the affirmative team normally parametricises down to a very specific subset of the topic, in order to limit the grounds of the debate. This is very similar to the purpose section of a feature specification. A great example of this sort of idea is when a software company chooses to add support for new technology to their product line. The purpose of the feature would generally explain the new technology and then narrowly define what the feature is targeting within the larger technological space.

Second, there is almost always a terminology section. Granted, this is not commonly found in affirmative cases anymore but traditionally was something you could almost always expect. The reason for its traditional inclusion in an affirmative case as well as in a software feature specification are to ensure all of the participants in the debate or design process have a common set of terms to use during the discussion. This is particularly compelling in very complex or unique positions wherein the terms being used may not be common knowledge.

Third, there is typically some form of acceptance criteria wherein the feature specification defines the criteria that will be used to determine the success or failure of the feature. This is obviously very similar to traditional LD debate wherein an explicit criterion is provided or to policy debate wherein the debaters appeal to particular judging paradigms in order to achieve success in the round.

Fourth, an obvious parallel with debate are the sections devoted to references, citations, and research. These serve several purposes in software design. They provide background, understanding, market analysis, and overall context around the feature. Additionally, they help explain why certain decisions were made or various design tradeoffs were deemed acceptable.

All of these of course feed into the acceptance criteria and overall design of the feature.

Perhaps the most important section of a feature specification is what is typically referred to as the detailed design. Sometimes this is broken out into separate high-level design and low-level design sections. Either way, the purpose of these sections have a direct relationship with their debate counterparts. In software design, this section provides an algorithm, data structures, and pseudo code to clearly explain how the problem will be solved. Often, this addresses alternative algorithms and their various advantages and disadvantages. These concepts translate pretty directly over into debate terminology.

The affirmative plan articulates a particular algorithm for solving a problem with a set of advantages over the status quo and a detailed explanation of the internal linkage within these arguments. Similarly, the negative team's counterplans and disadvantages are full of detailed algorithms and arguments with extensive logical analysis to refute the affirmative position. The whole debate round serves as a figurative manifestation of an overall feature specification wherein the various algorithms duke it out until the one most fitting the chosen criteria is selected.

Discourse

The need for discourse in the software development field is profound. By their nature, software developers love to design solutions to problems. The inevitable result of this is that if you ask ten software developers to each design a solution you will inevitably end up with ten radically different solutions. Whether the software company has a single software architect who makes all the decisions or all engineers are on an equal playing field and get to help drive decision-making, the need for discourse is equally vital. Having a firm background in debate is a key distinguishing attribute that can set an engineer apart and ensure their success and the success of the company they are part of.

Working for an early stage startup where all engineers have an equal voice in the overall design and implementation of a product drives a profound need for consensus-based decision-making. During my time in debate, I became intimately familiar with many feminist writings. As a male debater from the U.S. Air Force Academy, this usually arose when other teams ran the Feminism Kritik against us. As any good debater would, I pored through the literature. This study between tournaments and the discourse over feminism in debate rounds highlighted the importance of valuing multiple perspectives and diverse contributors in any project, meeting, or decision-making venture.

This was something that reframed how I approached the organization of our debate team, my leadership approach in the Air Force, and my team of software engineers. At SolidFire, we believe it is incredibly important to incorporate multiple voices in the design process. Thus, we strive to achieve consensus-based decisions as often as we can.

In that pursuit, there are several vital skills I learned in debate that uniquely prepared me for success in this role. First was the ability to articulate my ideas with a clear and logical explanation about the advantages and disadvantages. The importance of this cannot be overstated. In an early stage startup a lot of decisions are made between the core engineers discussing ideas and problems in person at a whiteboard rather than in meetings or over email. As such, the ability to verbally explain a position or perspective had immense value. Equally important was being able to intensely listen and critically analyze opposing perspectives. The most important skill of all was then the actual ability to *debate* and drive disagreements towards resolution. The way I drove disagreements towards consensus was by embracing ideals I learned in debate, such as John Stuart Mill's notion of The Marketplace of Ideas, wherein truth is strengthened and falsehoods abandoned as a result of the healthy exchange of ideas. Viewing disagreement *as a good thing* to drive us towards better solutions is something I attribute as one of our keys to success.

The other key debate principle that greatly shaped and influenced how I dealt with conflict and reached consensus was the idea of a false dichotomy fallacy. Often, when software developers disagree on approaches to a problem they wrongly view the disagreement as a dichotomy in which there is a forced choice between two extremes. In reality, this is rarely the case as we can often take parts of each approach and combine them into a new and improved solution that achieves the best of both worlds.

Any policy debater who has ever argued against a counter-plan has been richly prepared for avoiding this logical fallacy. The first line of argument against a counterplan almost always contains many different permutations of the affirmative plan text, which show that the plan and counterplan are not mutually exclusive, and can be combined in unique and different ways such that the policymaker doesn't have to choose between the two.

Finding and employing permutations between seemingly mutually exclusive solutions to software problems is one of the most critical tools in software development. This is particularly important for an early stage startup that is forced to make difficult decisions between time to market and solving problems in the ideal manner. In software development, we often face two dynamically opposed solutions. The first is typically very simple and easy to implement, but generally thought of as a hack with serious shortcomings in terms of scalability, flexibility, robustness, and long-term maintainability.

The second solution is typically the classically correct way to solve the problem as it will be more scalable, flexible, robust, and maintainable. Unfortunately, this solution is also usually substantially harder to implement, riskier to overall product stability, and requires substantially more test and validation. The most obvious debate inspired solution to this is a timeframe perm. Implement the first solution *now* in order to meet immediate time-to market-constraints and *in our next release,* implement the "right" solution. Escaping the forced choice fallacy and utilizing a timeframe perm allows an early stage startup to rapidly solve problems and beat larger companies to market, while still having an eye on the proper long-term solution to be distributed in the next release.

Another example illustrating the concept is a partial permutation, wherein parts of one plan are combined with parts of another plan in order to achieve an alternative with comparative net benefits over either of the original policy proposals. This concept is employed almost daily as a software engineer. Let's assume the same above scenario with the hack solution and the right solution. A partial permutation of those two approaches might pull in *parts* of the right solution and combine them with the hack solution to address the shortcomings of the original solution, while still keeping us under our scheduled deadline. Those portions of the right solution that are not pulled into the partial permutation solution can obviously still be deferred until the next release.

Above The Game Board

As a debater immersed in a round, it is easy to get caught up in the moment and the competition and care only about winning. The advent and increased popularity of kritiks in debate challenges our assumptions and mindsets and have lasting impacts on us as individuals, far outlasting our transient roles in debate. The practical skills debaters learn, as well as their philosophical approaches towards conflict and decision-making, prepare debaters for immense success in any career field. My experience as a software engineer over the last fifteen years helped me come to understand the most valuable lessons from debate regardless of one's chosen profession: the ability to research, critically analyze all sides of an argument, articulate and weigh the advantages and disadvantages, and ultimately engage in healthy discourse that drives disagreement towards consensus.

Marshall McMullen is a Principal Engineer at NetApp SolidFire. He has been in the software engineering field since 2001, which he entered into while serving as an officer in the United States Air Force. After graduate school, he spent several years honing his deep love and passion for C programming as a Kernel Developer for IBM. Afterwards he transitioned into parallel and distributed software development for the startup company LeftHand Networks, which was later acquired by Hewlett-Packard. In 2011, he became one of the original twelve founding members of SolidFire, Inc., which he helped lead to immense success and ultimate acquisition by NetApp in 2016. Marshall holds a B.S. in Legal Studies from the U.S. Air Force Academy (1998) and a M.S. in Computer Science from the University of Arizona (2003).

A Debater's Philosophy of Teaching

By Katy Bishoff

Elementary Educator

Competitive forensics has had a profound impact on my life in so many ways that it is a challenge to focus on one long enough to compose a coherent piece of writing about it. Each time I begin to think about a single facet of the activity, I'm flooded with memories of tournaments, peers, students. To spare you the inside jokes and emotion-filled tales, I'll instead try to convey the impact that forensics has had on my professional life.

First, I think it's important to explain what I had gained when I walked away from my time in forensics. A student I once coached wrote about forensics making him a better person because he had experienced being wrong. I think this perfectly encapsulates the character-change that we experience as debaters. Many come into the activity because they like to argue and want to get better at it, but the rounds that we learn the most from are often those that we lose. When one has experienced debate in an academic setting, one comes to understand that it is far more about hearing and valuing different perspectives than it is about being better at arguing.

You begin to see that even on ethical or policy decisions that seem to have an obvious right answer, there are always repercussions, disadvantages if you will, that require considera-tion. Thanks to my time as a debater, I am capable of having civil discussions with people who disagree with me on a very fundamental level on hot-button topics. This is because I understand that each unique perspective has equal value and regardless of their ability to change my mind, I will deepen my understanding of an issue simply by interacting with those who disagree.

These days, it is common to see people on any part of the political spectrum simply surrounding themselves with others who share their same opinions and not bothering to hear, or totally shutting down any dissent, so that they never grasp why anyone would disagree with them. My goal in life is to be the opposite of that person, to engage those who would oppose my views both for my own benefit, and to help them broaden their understanding as well.

In short, debate taught me how to be an informed and engaged member of the voting populace, something that I consider to be the most basic privilege and responsibility of adulthood. So when the time came for me to question what I wanted to do with my life to try and help the world be a better place, I decided that helping future generations fulfill that obligation was a worthwhile endeavor.

I'm an educator. As far as shaping responsible citizens, when one works in a secondary or post-secondary setting, it is easier to see a fairly immediate return on your investment so to speak because you are working with students who are already of voting age, or very close to it, and can understand the complexity of policy and decision-making. I, on the other hand, chose to work with primary students. Molding the minds of six-year-olds was where my heart led me. So how does one accomplish such a lofty goal before one's students have learned anything substantial about how our world works you might ask? That is a question I ask myself on a regular basis, "How am I helping these kids reach the end goal?"

The best answer I can usually give is that I'm laying the groundwork for what will come later. Sometimes in very simple ways, like helping them to become literate, the most basic skill that can increase one's civic engagement exponentially, or teaching them to add and subtract, something any financially independent adult will need to know. Sometimes however, I'm able to focus on skills more specific to the ideas of thinking critically and respecting dissent.

I took a professional development class recently during which we were asked to write down all of the things we want our students to know or be able to do when they graduate. It was incredibly encouraging to see that I was not alone among my staff. There were few academic skills on anyone's list. Instead, the lists were mainly composed of things like, be empathetic, think critically, work cooperatively, and respect others. If our school is any indication, educators today realize that while we have academic standards to meet, the far more important part of our job is to create functional citizens who will be marketable in a twenty-first century workforce, and willing and able to help solve our world's problems.

In the primary grades, children are still in the stage of development where they are moving from a self-centric view of the world to a broader understanding of the fact that other people experience the same emotions and struggles, or perhaps ones unique from their own. This is when they are able to begin to grasp how their own actions can affect others, a key time for guiding them to become empathetic actors. One of the latest crazes in the education world is Social-Emotional Learning (SEL), which happens to be a trendy way of saying, teach them to be self-aware and socially aware of emotions and interactions. Fortunately, this means that there are a lot of resources out there for ideas and activities for SEL in the classroom, because any good teacher knows it's better to borrow from another than to spend valuable prep time reinventing the wheel.

Much of SEL curriculum is finding ways for students to practice working cooperatively within the existing curriculum. For example, giving students a math problem with more than one potential method that will reach the correct solution. You could have students work in small groups so that they have to discuss and reach consensus on a method, or have students complete it independently, then discuss how. Either way this will help them to recognize a) that there is more than one perspective or way to solve and b) that each one is equally valuable because it resulted in the same correct answer. This is also an opportunity for students to practice explaining their thinking and showing that they can be respectful of another student doing the same, analyzing what they are explaining.

One of the first goals of SEL is to help students be able to identify emotions in themselves and others. I know it sounds basic, remember I have six-year-olds in my classroom, while also responding appropriately rather than reacting. Lessons that target these skills might involve role-playing so that students practice being both the one experiencing an emotion and the one causing it. This is building a foundation for the idea that one can only control oneself; sometimes people will do things that you feel negatively about, but one cannot control that, only one's own choice of how to respond to it.

I have dealt with some mind-bogglingly intense behavior problems in my class that test my own patience daily. I've found that even at this young age, they are capable of grasping this concept to the point that in a moment where they are so frustrated they are on the brink of reacting physically to provocation, they can in fact recognize that they have given their control to the other person and choose to ignore instead, taking back their power.

Perhaps it sounds at this point like we've veered off course a bit here. What does this have to do with debate? Well, what my kids are experiencing, and the situations in which they are able to apply those experiences, are very similar to how we learn to handle things in debate. When an opponent has brought up the same flawed argument that we've had countless neg teams throw at our case all year, and we just want to scream, our debate experience has taught us that this is not going to help us win the round. Better to calmly give it the briefest response we can, refuse to allow it to be a time-suck, and instead spend as much time as possible back on our own ground, talking about all of the wonderful advantages to our case or responding to other, more pertinent, attacks.

This translates to the real life skill of responding rather than reacting when you run into someone who disagrees with you and has what you consider to be the most ridiculous reasoning behind it. Getting frustrated isn't going to help, but calmly explaining to them why you believe that their reasoning is contradictory, based on a falsehood, or is missing an internal link, may actually have an impact.

Hopefully, the skills that we've been building in school from a young age will help them to do this with a cool head rather than becoming emotionally engaged. Not only does this skill allow students to be in control of themselves, it also helps them to view the world more empathetically. It teaches them to take the time to consider how someone else feels about a situation, and understand their perspective, before making a judgement.

The next step that I take is trying to introduce students to as many perspectives as possible. Just as we learn in debate that all voices are equally relevant, whether it be weighing an extinction impact against a kritik, or accepting that even when they vote against us for what feels like the wrong reasons, every judge has something important to teach us. This is the age when they are discovering how big the world is. They have a delightful, wide-eyed fascination every time I pull out the globe to explain where something is, because they're still trying to wrap their brains around the fact that our planet stretches far beyond any distance they have the perspective to truly understand. We read books about different cultures and discuss the similarities and differences from our own. We learn about how schools and houses look different in other countries, because these are the things they can relate to and compare to their own experiences.

When Martin Luther King Day happens, we engage in a conversation about what discrimination is and the fact that he was assassinated for his beliefs, rather than shying away from what some might consider a heavy topic for little kids. Yes, it's early and they deserve a childhood not burdened by the harshness of some realities, but I believe it's never too early to begin introducing people to concepts like equality that are so incredibly basic to our understanding of what it means to be human.

The final piece of this puzzle is that I want students to be able to gather information about something before forming an opinion or making a decision, so they will be able to make a reasoned argument to defend it. Someone who can do this will not fall victim to the sound-byte philosophies spewed by many news outlets. Unfortunately, the number of people who seem to be able to guard themselves against these tactics is dwindling.

In debate, we learn to do this because any argument that is "blippy" or can't stand up to an opponent's response is not strong enough to be considered on a judge's ballot. We later realize that this translates to our own ballot in real life when we vote. At age six, kids make few decisions for themselves, so the opportunities for building this skill look different than they would for a teenager; I simply seize every opportunity that presents itself.

What makes it a bit easier is that children at this age are naturally full of questions, frequently on the topic of "Why?" Often it's about something frivolous like, "Why is math in the morning today instead of the afternoon?" It sounds simple if you've never experienced having to calmly stop whatever you're doing for all twenty students, to respond to just one, especially when you know it's making everyone late for PE. It really forces you to fight the instinct to say, "Don't worry about it," and go back to what you were doing. By taking the time to stop and explain, I'm modeling for them that there should be an answer to every "Why?" and that they are doing the right thing by questioning it. If they don't understand why we do something the way we do, they deserve to hear the reasoning. It also demonstrates that things are not arbitrary, that every decision I've made about how we do things in the classroom is intentional and thought out in a way that I can defend when called upon to do so. Perhaps this model will encourage them to do the same as an adult, particularly when the time comes for them to be a parent.

Because we must encourage them to question! If we encourage it enough, perhaps they will continue to do so throughout their lives so that they won't accept things as being correct simply because they are status quo. I want them to be skeptical of anyone who can't convince them of the reasoning behind a why or isn't willing to entertain the challenge of a why.

In addition, on the occasions when I can allow things in our class to be decided through democratic process, we take the time to discuss the benefits and disadvantages of each option. When a first grader is presented with options like watch a movie or extra recess, they typically want to make a split second decision. Instead, I ask them to think about why they are inclined to vote for that option, perhaps ask them to share with others what their thinking is. Of course, we don't fit an entire policy debate round into this time, but it is a chance for kids to start thinking about their rationale behind a decision and practice being able to articulate it, potentially even convincing others to change their own opinion. This is what informed voting looks like in first grade. It's not much, but it's a starting point.

At the end of the day, I hope that students walk away from my classroom with a better ability to identify and handle emotion, value and seek out other perspectives, keep asking "Why?" and be able to explain their own choice. And who knows, maybe they'll be drawn to debate when they reach secondary and continue to hone their skills to be the most well informed and engaged citizens they can possibly be. But even if they don't, I'll feel secure in the fact that I've done what I can to help them reach that end point, maybe making the world a slightly better place.

Katy Bishoff is an elementary school teacher for the Anchorage School District in Girdwood, Alaska. She participated in high school forensics, competing in interpretation of literature and policy debate. Beginning in 2008, she returned to her alma mater as an assistant coach while earning a degree in education. Upon taking her current position in Girdwood, she could no longer coach at the high school level but still remained involved in the forensics community as a volunteer. In addition to her teaching duties, she also works with Girdwood's middle school debaters.

Section IV: Engaged Citizenship

If debate did nothing more than create a social network for students and prepare them for the challenges of college and beyond, that would be more than enough to justify its inclusion in our schools. However, the importance of debate extends far beyond the benefits to the individual competitor.

Participants in academic debate learn that there is more to life than what they see in their limited personal sphere of experience. It makes them aware of the realities of the world. It opens their eyes to injustice. Debate teaches them empathy. It teaches them that the issues confronting us as a nation, as global citizens are rarely black and white, that there are no absolutes, that the other's perspective has value.

It teaches them how to advocate for themselves and others.

The following essays highlight the efforts of debaters to leave a meaningful mark on the society of which they are a part.

Debate as Theater of Social Change

By Matt Stannard

Policy Director at Commonomics USA

After coaching debate for 15 years, I entered the world of public policy advocacy: researching problems and proposals, writing position papers and drafting model laws, orating and arguing my organizations' positions, and coaching activists on argumentative and political strategies. The skills portability from academic debate to legal and policy reform work is easy to see. Debaters come to implicitly understand ethos as a combination of preparation and performance. Research, preparation, listening, refutation, and comparison are academic debate's skill analogs to public discourse. Because of this, I know hundreds of public office-holders, attorneys, and professional agitators who debated. Debate gave us an edge.

But something else dwells in the world of public policy advocacy, something below the surface of, or always encircling, the professional rules and norms of public service and the policymaking process. Where one expects to find reasoned conversation about competing policy proposals, one finds advocates playing power games behind the scenes that condition the ability of various stakeholder groups to get into the room in the first place. Policy professionals' need for funding and institutional support functions as a gatekeeper for proposals that uphold predominant power relationships. Classism, racism, sexism, and various layers of privilege interact in a world of chronic insecurity. Because of this, the best proposals don't always win the day. What can experience in academic debate inform us about navigating a world rife with inequality and distorted communication?

As a competitive academic game, debate *ideally* rewards advocacy informed by research, listening, and comparison. Players take turns, follow rules, and debate about some of those rules. To an extent, competitors must adapt to the stylistic and argumentative preferences of their judges (insofar as those are known), and so the game also rewards a certain amount of empathy and an ability to articulate arguments in ways that make sense to others.

There are ethical lessons embedded in the game too: we cannot ignore our opponents' arguments, and in fact, to respond appropriately to them, we must strive to understand them at least partially from their point of view. For half of the debate, we have no choice but to listen to them, and the better we listen, the better we can respond. In close debates, judges will reward a nuanced representation of the truth of our opponents' arguments weighed against our own, rather than an unfair dismissal of them. Debate rewards a proactive attentiveness— an ethical gesture as much as a strategic one.

Then there is academic debate's nuanced treatment of rules. Debate is rule-based, but many of the rules are subject to argument and interpretation. Competitors make arguments about what their opponents should and should not be allowed to do. Engaging in such conversations helps students understand the norms—communicative, legal, and procedural—that govern civic engagement, law, and policymaking.

Participants learn that rules both govern and are subject to interpretation, are both determinative and ever-changing, articulated and unstable. Former debaters will find these paradoxical truths about rulemaking when they take a civil procedure class in law school, or learn about administrative and agency rulemaking, or try to run a nonprofit board meeting or a town council hearing.

Above all, because it is a game, the skills that debate rewards will be maximized in the skill sets of participants. They will emerge from debate with superior critical thinking skills, the creativity to imagine causal chains and anticipate unintended consequences, the ability to read complex literature for the purpose of finding cogent arguments, the thickness-of-skin to listen to others passionately disagree with them, the understanding of both the necessity and mutability of rules, and the wisdom that comes from learning, again and again, that being correct in one's own mind is insufficient; that what is important is to appear credible and correct to others. All of these skills and lessons transpose into engaged civic life, whether former debaters devote their entire careers to legal and political advocacy, or whether they use those skills to periodically engage as members of their communities on issues that concern them.

This is all very important. But notice I began by using the word *ideally*. Debate *ideally* rewards this hard work, attentiveness, audience empathy, ethical commitment to listening, and fair representation. And even when debate doesn't fully live up to those ideals, it still tends to produce those skills. But in order to understand the whole picture of how academic debate prepares us for public and civic engagement, we need to dwell more attentively on its failures: Material power imbalances and the prejudices and hierarchies of real life have problematized the potential of this rule-based communication game to conduct itself equitably and empower its participants equally. Over the past several years, American policy debate has ruthlessly, with precision (and a lot of resistance), criticized itself. Its practitioners and educators have discovered that many of the competitive and stylistic norms are not race-, gender-, or class-neutral; that many of the ways we've facilitated debate education and competition have privileged the same groups and classes that historically dominate academic, political, and civic life.

For most of its history, American policy debate did not explicitly confront these power imbalances or acknowledge them in its form and content. Philosophically, participants mostly assumed that the point of the game was to introduce and defend a good idea. Performatively, participants mostly assumed that the rules and norms of debate (including the more esoteric norms of speaking style and research burdens) benefitted all participants equally. Once the debate community actually began to confront these issues, the form and content of competitive debates evolved rapidly—often awkwardly—into new sets of argumentative and performative norms.

This evolution is still taking place. Debaters will raise questions of oppression and identity—race, gender, sexuality, disability—as framework-level issues to be used as mechanisms to evaluate procedural and substantive arguments. They might analyze the political economy of policymaking in order to point out that they aren't really roleplaying as policymakers. They might point out that the think tanks, scholars, and corporate media that make up policy debate's literature base are mired in ideological biases. They might even challenge the esoteric communicative norms of rapid delivery as exclusive and socially aloof. In some instances, debaters might do none of these things, choosing instead to advocate a policy reform and answer pragmatic objections to their advocacy. But all participants in American policy debate at any given tournament or in any given pre-season topic discussion might expect to engage in any or all of these new, critical variances.

But aren't these new approaches a destructive departure from the skill-building necessary for civic engagement and political activism? In fact, they aren't. These variances stem from inequalities. Confronting those inequalities in debate can help us understand the messy and capricious power relationships of real social and political life. American policy-style debaters, in particular, have cultivated a new set of stylistic approaches and argumentative themes that are self-reflective and critical of institutional power and cultural exclusion. Because debate is performative and not merely analytic—that is, because participants perform their arguments—structure can exist alongside critique of structure, rules and conventions simultaneously followed and unfollowed.

As a self-conscious, political theater performatively articulating socially relevant arguments, academic debate reminds me of the dramatic theories and political theaters of Bertolt Brecht and Augusto Boal. Brecht and Boal both developed their theories of drama, and their creation of innovative theaters, in times and places of severe material inequality and political repression. In Germany in the 1920s and 1930s, Brecht fought against the rise of fascism by developing a dramatic theory of egalitarian political empowerment. He believed that performance should spark and facilitate rational self-reflection and political education in the audience. By viewing dramatic production as a collective construction rather than a mere fantasy, Brecht believed audiences might see their own collective reality as constructed and, therefore, changeable through collective democratic action.

In Brazil in the 1950s and 1960s, when the country was on the brink of military takeover, Augusto Boal evolved Brecht's self-conscious political theater into a theater of the oppressed, including a breakdown of distinctions between actor and audience. He fashioned a type of theatrical experience where spectators became actors, setting out to determine the solutions to social and political problems presented in the productions. Both Brecht and Boal fled and eventually returned to their home countries, and both pursued these radically democratic visions of theater-as-argumentation throughout their lives.

Like those radical performative theatrics, academic debate is a self-conscious, performative articulation of social arguments, and as such a game, has the potential to open and cultivate performative argumentative norms in spaces that are not universally available in our civic and political life. Political theater has been vital in revolutionary communities because it offers participants a space to articulate and perform critique and change. In transparent and deliberative ways, mindful of the need for reciprocity between the participants themselves, and between participants and audience, both policy debate and political theater create spaces not only to learn about the nuts and bolts of politics, but also inequalities and injustices, and strategies for overcoming them. Political theater and policy debate—when committed to both intellectual rigor and openness to criticism—provide space for advocates to better understand both the injustices and the emancipatory potentials of public life.

Some debate educators are not keen on the recent critical and highly politicized turn of academic debate. While many of their concerns are understandable, they may be off the mark. To thrive, live justly, and cooperate in the complex decades to come, people will need to walk the line between reform and revolution, knowing when to work within systems and when to question them and agitate for their reinvention. Exercises of power and talent must be informed by solidarity with the powerless. Protest and revolt must be informed by knowing how systems work and policies are implemented. Academic debate's tension between rule-based conventions and boundary-pushing criticism ought to remain unresolved, reason and revolt theatrically juxtaposed. That juxtaposition is civic engagement in a nutshell.

Matt Stannard coached college debate for 15 years, including 11 years as Director of Forensics at the University of Wyoming, where his teams won National Parliamentary Debate Association (NPDA) and National Parliamentary Tournament of Excellence (NPTE) national championships and made National Debate Tournament (NDT) and Cross Examination Debate Association (CEDA) elimination round appearances. In 2009, he and five other coaches travelled to Iraq to lead the first debate workshop in that country, at the University of Duhok. After receiving a JD from University of Wyoming's College of Law, Matt began a career in public advocacy, working for causes including domestic violence shelter and outreach, banking reform, and sustainable economies. He is finishing his first book, The American Commons, and writes on economic and political issues for several publications. He is policy director for Commonomics USA and a member of the Public Banking Institute's board of directors.

Debating in the Public Sphere

By Steve Johnson

Director of Debate at the University of Alaska Anchorage

A presidential election year is a great opportunity to take stock of the state of debate in the republic. With national primaries followed by a general election, there's no shortage of events billed as debates to consider and, perhaps more importantly, people are keenly interested in debating because of this. Whether considering matchups between preferred candidates or criticizing the events themselves, each presidential election presents opportunities to evaluate the health of debating in our republic.

I'm confident in saying the majority of academic debate coaches would rate the health of our activity as quite good, particularly when compared to what passes for debates between competing presidential candidates. Unfortunately, I'm not as confident that the general public recognizes any difference between what happens between those candidates and what our students study and compete in weekend after weekend.

Much of this is our own fault. As tournament debating has become the default mode of interaction for debate programs, we have—for a variety of reasons—increasingly sequestered ourselves from the general public. Our tournaments are very frequent (nearly every weekend throughout the academic year) and happen throughout the country, but they're not designed to be accessible to the public. Multiple rounds scheduled simultaneously; rounds scheduled in far-flung buildings in uncomfortable spaces; limited and transient information about who is debating when, what, and where; numerous rounds happening on inhumane schedules over the course of multiple days; culminating rounds scheduled for late in the evening; and a general preference for efficiency over receptiveness make clear that we are not interested in bringing the public to our events. To be clear: each of these characteristics is justified by pursuit of a worthy goal: increasing the number of students who may benefit from debating and maximizing the efficiency and efficacy of the tournament experience, but it is undeniable that these characteristics make tournaments less than hospitable for laypersons.

The consequences of this approach are easily discernable: the public has little to no conception of what it is we do or what reasoned discourse over public policy as practiced by academic debating looks like. This must change. Between growing pressures on funding for higher education and a general abuse of "debate" to refer to events that resemble nothing approaching reasoned, thoughtful exchange, there's no time to waste in re-involving the general public in academic debating. To fail to do so is to fiddle while Rome burns.

The University of Alaska Anchorage's Seawolf Debate Program has undertaken a project over the last ten years to reconnect with our various communities in ways that establish us as a leader in the promotion of civil discourse. In this chapter, I lay out the principles that guide that project and offer examples of how we put those principles into action.

Principle 1: Create events that are welcoming and engaging

The most important effort that a debate program can make is to design events that the general public wants to attend, either as participants or audience members. Chief among the ways to accomplish this is to create events that are welcoming to the public. Most members of the public don't think of debating as a season of competition or a weekend chock-full of rounds, but of debate as a discrete event. Consider how often we are approached by a community observer with a question of "is this where the debate is happening?" As coaches, competitors, and tournament directors, we are usually immersed in the tournament experience and quickly respond with a "yes" or "who are you looking for?" More importantly, consider the specific choice of language used by those who wander into our tournaments: "*the* debate." Capitalizing on this expectation is the first secret of designing accessible events.

The Seawolf Debate Program organizes almost all of our civic events around this principle: we create events with the expressed intention of attracting members of the public. We choose days and times that are likely to attract an audience, host in venues that the public enjoys patronizing, and involve them in ways beyond passive spectating.

Consider the 2015 U.S. Universities Debating Championships hosted by the University of Alaska Anchorage. While this event was a typical competitive tournament in many ways, we went to great lengths to make the event accessible to the public. We designated one room as the most publicly-accessible venue for the event: that room was comfortable (it used to house a pub on our campus), centrally located (it was in the same building as the tournament headquarters), featured an interpretive staff (who explained to the audience what they could expect going into a debate round and answered questions at the conclusion of each debate), and always featured the top ranked teams in the competition.

We usually had an audience of more than twenty people for each preliminary round, far more than what typically attends an average preliminary round at any given tournament. Beyond the efforts to make the preliminary rounds accessible, our promotion for the championship (which was considerable—we had a partnership with several media companies in town who ran ads for us) focused on the final round of the tournament. This round was scheduled for the early evening and was held in a large theatre on campus. We successfully attracted approximately 350 members of the public to an event for which they did not know (at least while we were promoting the round in advance of the competition) which universities would be represented nor even what the topic would be.

Which leads to another way to communicate the value of attending debate rounds to the public: selling tickets. This is anathema to some who lead debate programs, particularly those who direct programs at public universities. I understand this reluctance, but the old adage that an event is worth what you charge for it is particularly true for debating. Not only does selling tickets communicate the value of an event, it increases the commitment people have to attend that event, all while raising valuable funds for debate programs.

Finally, a critical part of successful events is involving the audience beyond the level of spectators. There are many tried and true ways to do this, ranging from floor speeches to question-and-answer sessions during or after the debate. One of the most useful ways we've found to involve the audience is to allow them to express their opinion on the motion.

Using a service called PollEverywhere.com, we ask the audience to submit via text message their opinion about the motion before and after each of our public debates. These opinions are recorded on a bar graph that updates dynamically as each audience member texts his or her opinion in. We compare the audience's attitude before and after the debate to award the win to the side that caused the greatest change in the audience's attitude from pre- to post-debate. There are manifold other ways to incorporate technology into these events so that the audience feels more involved: Twitter feeds, live blogging, encouraging audience members to share their opinions and arguments on Facebook, and the like all extend the audience's involvement beyond their simple witnessing of the debate.

Principle 2: Focus on issues people care about

Debating is a powerful way to encounter the world precisely because it focuses on controversies in which people feel they have a stake. Designing an effective public event requires that you select topics that focus on these very controversies.

Fortunately, the various extemporaneous formats of debate that are gaining popularity in the United States now create a great deal of familiarity with focusing on controversial current events. Student debaters, should they be the main participants in your event, will find it relatively easy to take the skills learned in competition into a public debate on an issue that, because of its local or temporal significance, attracts significant audience interest.

But public debates between students are not the only option available to directors who want to diversify the outreach component of their programs. The Seawolf Debate Program has had great success with a new series of debates featuring advocates who are policymakers or policy experts exchanging points of view in the academic debating format. We call our ongoing event the Arguing Alaska Debate Series and host debates quarterly at a local theater pub that sells high quality craft beer and delicious food. We partnered with our state newspaper to choose topics and recruit advocates that we know will attract public attention. We now regularly sell out a 400 seat theatre at $15 per ticket for these debates.

Our efforts to form partnerships to address controversial current events are not limited to this one event. The State of Alaska is currently facing a serious fiscal crisis precipitated by a sharp and sudden decline in the price of crude oil, the primary source of revenue for the state. In response, we have partnered with a local philanthropic foundation with a mandate to inform the public on current events issues to produce a year-long public debate tournament on the more controversial proposals to address the state's fiscal uncertainty. This contest, open to all high school and university students in the state, will begin with video submissions of examples of oral advocacy from which the top competitors will be selected to attend an in-person tournament later in the year.

Principle 3: Assume a leadership role in promoting civil discourse

Perhaps the most important undertaking for a debate program director seeking to reconnect to the public is to stake out a leadership position in the advancement of civil discourse within your university and surrounding community. Beyond the obvious efforts to make oneself available to others as an authority on public argument, there are two broad areas in which a director so inclined may assert himself or herself as an expert.

Perhaps most important is to take your debate instruction beyond your own squadroom. While this is intuitive for most—given the vast majority of directors of debate are also faculty members—opportunities to instruct may be found in many places. The first step in promoting this principle is to imagine debate not merely as an extra- or co-curricular activity, but as a discreet pedagogy, no different than an essay or an oral report. These fundamental tools, common to a majority of classrooms, are so pervasive that they need no justification. Debate, on the other hand, is often perceived as too complex, too technical, or too intimidating. Adapting our practices to provide a reasonable balance between accessibility and rigor will go a long way toward creating a product that can be marketed to colleagues as an assignment that is both productive and manageable.

In addition to expanding your teaching beyond the classroom, there exist many opportunities to serve as a leader in designing forums and practices of effective civil discourse. Rotary groups, chambers of commerce, political parties, and the like routinely host debates between candidates and on issues. Proactively approaching entities such as this with an offer to contribute to the success of their efforts is usually received very favorably.

At one recent event, I was successful at convincing our local chamber of commerce to take a risk and depart from the typical managed press conference approach to a political candidates' debate. I worked with the chamber and both candidates to identify three issues that were expressed as propositions to be debated; designed a brief debate format that allowed time for construction, engagement, and rebuttal; and hosted three mini-debates in the course of one and one-half hours.

Followed by audience text-based voting, these debates were more focused, engaging, and interactive than any of the manifold other events in which the candidates participated. Anecdotal reports from both the candidates and audience members indicate that the approach was a welcome improvement over the status quo.

Regardless of variations on any of these approaches, it seems obvious that debating has the capacity to go well beyond the limited approach that dominates our activity. Imagination, creativity, and determination to return debate to its rightful place in the public sphere are all that are needed to create events that are simultaneously enjoyable and illuminating for the public to whom we should be responsive.

Steve Johnson has been active in competitive academic debating for three decades, coaching teams of nationally and international-ly successful debaters. He has been involved in the development or expansion of a number of formats of debating, always searching for balance between rigorous competition and public accessibility. His most recent effort has been to expand the mandate of the University of Alaska Anchorage's Seawolf Debate Program to promote civil discourse in his community.

The Seawolf Debate Program's Community Outreach

The following examples are just some of the ways the Seawolf Debate Program at the University of Alaska Anchorage (featured in the preceding chapter) has fostered an ethic of civil discourse in the city of Anchorage and state of Alaska.

- Organize and administer the region's Middle School Debate Program
- Encourage debaters and staff to serve as paid or volunteer coaches for high school programs
- Serve as volunteer judges at local high school tournaments
- Run a high school tournament in a format not offered in the area
- Host the high school Drama, Debate, & Forensics State Championship
- Host an intramural debate tournament for non-debate team members at the university; debate team members/alumni serve as coaches and judges
- Hold exhibition debates for local groups such as faculty development organizations, rotary clubs, etc.
- Hold public scrimmages with visiting university debate teams
- Host debate watches during the election cycle

- Organize pop-up debates for community members at local coffee shops; team members serve as moderators for the event

- Moderate political candidate debates

- Organize debates between experts in the field on issues of local significance

The Patients' Advocate

By Sarah Garwood, MD

Pediatrician

She had remained composed during most of the office visit, but when I caught her in the hallway before re-entering her 14-year-old child's room, Serena's face fell. "I don't think she's safe at school... I 'm so afraid" she whispered. I froze and then replied with one of the standard prompts in my line of work as an Adolescent Medicine physician. "Tell me more."

Lucy's mother and I had a strong rapport and history by the time she spoke aloud her terror for her transgender child. Born as Luke, Lucy was biologically male but since a toddler had persistently insisted that she was actually a girl. At first her mother hoped it was a phase. After all, Serena's friends, family, and pediatrician all reassured her that it most certainly had to be. Instead, as she grew, Lucy became more distressed and finally, frankly depressed by the pressure to continue living as a boy.

Eventually Lucy's parents came to the conclusion that she was transgender, and began the process of allowing her to transition to a female gender role. Some of the rewards were immediate. Lucy was happier and seemed to be thriving in school and with her peers. However, since entering high school, even though she had made several friends, things seemed off. She had become withdrawn and had quit her after-school art club. The week prior, another parent contacted Serena because a classmate confided that she was upset by name-calling she saw online directed at Lucy. Some of the posts threatened physical violence and said that the "She-Man" should not be allowed in school.

We completed our clinic visit that day with the expected screenings for depression, suicidal thoughts, cutting behavior; assessment of coping strategies; suggestions for therapy and support groups; and a general pep talk. As Lucy walked out the door doing her best to give me a brave smile, our eyes met and an understanding passed between us. Everything we had just talked about was not enough. In a world where state legislatures are codifying discrimination in laws, where people of "faith" routinely publicly state that you have no place in this world, and where your biggest worry every day is whether you will be harassed or humiliated at school while you try to just pass as an average kid, motivational speeches by your doctor fall unbearably short.

I carry patients like Lucy with me. I entered medicine to be a healer, but how can I ease this sort of suffering? When I read medical journals, when I watch the news, when I talk to parents, I do these things with Lucy beside me, prodding me to answer that question. In the case of transgender kids, one promising solution is called "LGBT inclusive sexual health education," which is basically sex ed that takes into account the reality that not everyone is heterosexual or cis-gendered. When my local school district decided to step out as a leader in this area and move a few steps in the direction of comprehensive sexual health education, which was more inclusive of LGBT kids, I was encouraged and proud to live in the district.

Sadly, my enthusiasm was short-lived, as the community backlash that followed was swift, organized, and impassioned. Emails with template letters drafted were distributed and a document with a list of arguments against gender identity was circulated as the backbone of the dissent. At first I observed with amusement. This feeling turned to shock and anger as school board members began expressing doubts about passing the curricular changes. The vote was delayed for six months due to the controversy.

Like-minded parents and community members in support of the changes rallied together and sized up the situation. There was a battle before us. Vulnerable kids needed us to be a voice of support for them. We would have to find a way to speak up for what we believed to be right based on reason, logic, and evidence. To do that, we would need a strategy. We would also need storytelling and charisma. We would need to address the arguments the opposition presented and neutralize them. In short, we would need to prepare for a debate match.

It has been twenty years since I have participated in or witnessed a debate match, but there was a time in my life when I ate, slept, and breathed this activity. I loved the fast-paced, think-on-your-feet, adrenaline rush of tracking and defeating your opponent's arguments. I remember the focused concentration it took to remain calm, confident, and level-headed as you were cross-examined. The poker face you held even while you knew your opponent had found the area of vulnerability in your armor.

My experiences in high school debate helped give me the confidence, presence, and poise to walk into this battle on behalf of my patients and other kids like them. The stakes were higher than a trophy or bragging rights, though. I was reminded of what Veronica Roth wrote, "No matter how long you train someone to be brave, you never know if they are or not until something real happens." I knew the reality: discrimination and stigma literally kill people, and I felt the weight of that as I walked into every school board meeting for six months to present a citizen's statement. I felt it during media interviews and when I spoke on an expert panel to the school board.

Luckily, I was able to call on the cool, resolute, neutral stare I had practiced for hundreds of hours as a teenager in debate when, years later, I was personally targeted by neighbors and former friends for my advocacy. While I was not under the delusion that these curriculum changes would prevent all bullying of LGBT kids, or that somehow there would no longer be bathroom debates on the news, I hoped these changes would lead to a domino effect among other districts in the region.

Fortunately, all the efforts of the many parents and community members paid off and the school board passed the curriculum changes. People on both sides of the issue shook hands, packed up their files, and moved on. While the experience was undoubtedly stressful, I did not walk away feeling spent. Instead, revisiting the skills I gained in debate gave me renewed energy to use those skills when I have opportunities to be a voice for kids.

For my patients like Lucy, solutions will continue to be found outside my clinic exam room. As a physician, I know that my patients need more than routine appointments can give them. As a former debater, I know that there are a plethora of options on the table if you take the time to research them, develop them, and present them clearly. As a medical provider, I hope I can join those two aspects of my life in order to find the solutions my patients need and the courage to be the advocate they deserve.

Sarah Garwood is a board certified pediatrician, specializing in adolescent medicine. She is an Assistant Professor in the Pediatrics Division of Adolescent Medicine and the Associate Program Director for the Pediatric Residency Program at the Washington University School of Medicine in St. Louis. She is also the Medical Director of the SPOT at Jennings High School, the first comprehensive School Based Health Center in St. Louis County. Her areas of clinical interest are medical conditions affecting adolescents, including teen-age eating disorders, weight management, adolescent depression, anxiety, sexually transmitted diseases, reproductive health, and sexual identity. She is consistently recognized in "The Best Doctors in America" list compiled by Best Doctors, Inc.

Breaking My Silence

By Thomas D. Allison, Esq.

President, Social Justice Advocacy Project, Inc.

There is torture in silence, especially forced silence. When I talk about silence, I mean real silence, a type of silence that persists even when speaking. This is the silencing of our souls. Our desire for expression is innate and natural. However, norms, rules, and social conventions silence countless individuals and prevent them from expression. What debate has meant for me is simple: it has helped end my silencing and provided me the ability to create my own platform.

I believe in Plato and Aristotle's notion that we are all programmed with an essence, something that makes us who we are; I believe that essence is purpose. Everyone needs a voice, a voice that is suitable to allow people to realize their purpose. Dr. King reminded us that "a riot is the language of the unheard," and we know from history that people are willing to die for a voice in fulfillment of their purpose.

I believe in one's right to achieve fulfillment of their true calling, as I feel compelled to action on various issues, even where action appears blatantly futile. One issue where I feel such compulsion is social justice. My experience in life and the compulsion I feel leads me to believe my essence, my purpose, is social justice advocacy. As a social justice advocate, I need a voice that permits me to engage in effective advocacy against social injustice, wherever I may be of influence. While the necessity of having an appropriate voice was always clear to me, the realization of my calling as a social justice advocate came later.

Finding My Voice

I was born in Los Angeles, California, to a single mother, whom eventually had two more boys with my stepfather. Being a single mother, disabled, with three boys, my mother was not in a position to provide the security she would have wanted. I grew up in poverty and did not have the luxuries many of my friends had; sometimes these luxuries included milk for cereal, if there was cereal. At an early age, I began to do what I could to provide my family the security we needed, which included mowing lawns and doing odd jobs until I was able to gain legal employment at my first job as a cook and cashier at Kentucky Fried Chicken. Growing up with little to nothing permitted me to take pride in things that were not material, including the results of my labor.

Amidst growing up poor, my mother encouraged us to stay active and participate in as much as we could. As a young boy, I become heavily involved in my church. I would volunteer to address the congregation when given the opportunity and was invited several times to speak. Once I became a deacon as a teenager, these occurrences happened more formally and frequently. Though I enjoyed preaching to crowds and expressing my beliefs, even as a child, I knew there was something more to say, something more to do, and much more to aspire to. I was speaking, but I was not using *my* voice. These realizations practically taunted me as a child. I constantly contemplated life, the nature and quality of our existence, and the philosophical problem of evil (although I was not aware of "the problem of evil" as a formal consideration of philosophy).

Many nights I lay awake all night, contemplating various aspects of our existence. I understand now why Aristotle opines the young are unequipped to be students of philosophy, as the lack of experience restricts the depth one is able to go in their thought. I found my inquiries to be compulsive, but torturous and unfulfilling.

While I did not grow up with material possessions, I remember always having books. The Internet was not something we could use for information, it barely existed as far as I was aware. If my brothers or I had questions about things, my mother would often respond with: "go look it up." If it was important enough to us, we would. Because my mother did not allow me to play football until I got to high school, I researched every aspect of the game that was included in the books we had. Many times we could not even afford milk for our cereal, *yet we had these books.*

The constant presence of reading material, even though I did not like reading, made education an important factor in our household. Although my mother did not finish vocational college, she always inspired in us a motivation to produce our best work. For this reason, despite the environment I grew up in and the things I went without, my aspirations superseded my needs and desires. I could not participate in something without leaving my mark, as my mother puts it, even to present day.

My childhood, though lacking, was better than many people I know who had everything. Being poor reinforced my ability to dream. When you grow up without things, you have plenty of time to imagine the things you would want. Since the probability of achieving anything seems improbable, why not go all the way if it is only a dream? That is the way I saw the world. This is also something I can credit my mother for: she is a dreamer. She taught us to dream and think big, even though our circumstances were not always stable. Living and thinking this way showed me a part of the world and gave me experiences that my colleagues now would pay to have. For these things, I am extraordinarily grateful.

However, despite the course of my life through high school, I was missing something. The lack of voice began to grow evident, as I continued to torture myself with notions that an existentialist would consider absurd, notions like who are we? What is our purpose? How do we fulfill them? What type of power does man actually have in the realm of our existence? These thoughts reinforced a depth of life for me that required me to seek action or solutions. I was missing something, I knew I was missing something, but I had no idea what it was.

Once I entered college, I became aware of what I had been without my whole life. I attended a small university, the University of La Verne, which permitted me to make friends and continue through, though the road was far from easy. I met people who not only had material possessions, but also the advice and guidance from professional parents who had navigated the very journey their children were on. My mother did her best, but her best was restricted to what I had already been exposed to, although her life experience proved more than fruitful in my professional development. Understanding the deficit between what I knew and what the other students knew was depressing, but not defeating. Through my interactions with friends and peers, coupled with traveling for football games, I was becoming more and more aware of how much bigger the world was compared to my previous understanding—both geographically and socially. The more I learned, the lesser I felt. I know knowledge has a way of minimizing a person, especially when the person does not know what to do with the knowledge.

Introduction to Debate

During the spring semester of my junior year in college, I was having dinner in the on-campus cafeteria with a young lady whom I considered to be both smart and attractive. We debated cereal, silly I know, but I had her attention. This young lady then invited me to debate practice this coming Friday night. "Debate? On a Friday night? Who would do that to themselves?" was my response. I had no idea formal debate actually existed aside from urban legend. She implored me to go and agreed to sit next to me during practice and have dinner with me on a different occasion. Although the dinner never happened, I went to debate practice that Friday evening and sat next to her. We discussed the round afterward and of course I had a few suggestions for the debaters (as everyone does who is not actively part of the debate).

My response prompted her to disclose my ideas to the coach, Professor (now Dean) Ian Lising. Ian invited me to speak at the next practice, but like everyone else not actively part of the debate, I declined in nervousness and humility. This did not last long.

I started attending practice regularly and eventually joined in on debate rounds. Although I initially lost all of my rounds, my competitive spirit would not let me quit and being a sore loser would not permit me to continue losing. In losing, however, there was plenty of learning. Debate gained my respect because it was not easy and the people I practiced against did not make it easy.

One of my biggest issues was grammar. I could not speak with proper grammar and it was a distraction, including to me, causing me to correct myself, mid-speech, disrupting the flow and persuasion of my public address. Despite all of my struggles, after hard work and dedication, I would go on to advance to elimination rounds in over thirty tournaments, more than twenty final rounds, and win seven championships. I was the top ranked debater in four tournaments and was a 2008 United States Universities Debating Championship Finalist. I have competed in more than ten states and four countries and attribute much of my professional success to my debate career.

If I could go back and convince myself to join debate earlier, I would. Getting a head start on the benefits I have realized could have only made my life better. This is the advice I would give myself.

Why Debate?

Relationships. Debate has provided me a diversity of relationships, from some of my best friends to my wife. The debate circuit is the only place one would have an opportunity to meet an incredibly diverse group of people. I participated in British Parliamentary debate, a style of debate that is an international activity, encompassing people from a number of different races, classes, and cultures. For the first time in my life, I had experienced privileged white individuals who were afraid to argue with me. Through its unique structure and demands on individuals, debate has the ability to be an equalizer.

After you battle in round, you exit the room and allow the adjudicators to decide rankings and speaker points. This is the best moment to make friends because everyone's guard is down due to the vulnerability caused by impending judgment. Everyone is equal because in most rounds the rankings are not exactly clear, and most individuals want to take their mind off of the anxiety caused by awaiting a potential loss. Debate gives you the opportunity to know people that you would otherwise never encounter. These relationships set the stage for vigorous competition and create a far-reaching network.

Competition. As I have mentioned before, debate is the great equalizer. As a black man, I had a unique life story compared to my competition, which would often lend itself to a unique world perspective. A debate about poverty is different for someone who has lived it compared to someone who has only studied it. I won every single public benefits debate I debated in, no matter the tournament nor the competition. It is one thing to read about or envision living in poverty and actually experience not knowing where your next meal would come from. Utilizing my life experiences, learning the lessons of public speaking, and developing my alter ego put me in a position to succeed.

About my alter ego: whenever I take on a monumental task at school or work or when debating something I thought was advanced, I would shut down. Having been raised without much and knowing there was so much I had not learned, like basic grammar, I had to fight through a lack of confidence. These issues can be debilitating; however, I realized that no individual I was performing in front of knew me, and neither did they know my story. They had no idea who I was, what I knew, or what I had experienced.

Any restrictions caused by my past were self-inflicted as the people I spoke and performed in front of were unaware of my past. I learned that I could be whoever I wanted to be in front of fellow debaters and judges and they would never know whether it was real or not. I decided that when I was in front of people, I would be "Big T." Big T is the Man. Big T is better looking than Denzel Washington, more articulate than Dr. King, smarter than Socrates, and more passionate than Malcolm X. With these skills, who could be better? This mentality got me through many speeches and debates, with resounding applause. I literally had nothing to lose, but everything to gain.

The substance of my core is informed by my life experiences, both the positive and the negative. Debating poverty takes a different meaning when it is a part of your identity. Debating gangs and crime is one thing, but having held a gun for the first time in fear for my safety at age eleven gives true perspective. Debating empowering the poor is one thing, but another when you are poor and empowered. Had I not suffered and gone without, I would not have had the substance that made me successful at debate. Debate taught me how to use my story not only to win rounds, but also to craft my personal narrative that impacts everything I do to this day. When people ask me: "how have you been able to succeed despite your struggle?" I respond: "I have only been able to succeed because of my struggle." Being poor puts you in a position of having nothing to lose. This is a weapon in itself, but knowledge is what gives even the most disenfranchised power.

Thirst for knowledge. Nothing has inspired me to want to learn more than losing a debate round, one debate round in particular. On multiple occasions I had the opportunity to compete at a debate tournament with my good friend Dr. John Patrick (a relationship formed through debate over ten years ago). On one occasion, John and I were at a debate tournament where we got first place in four of the five rounds of that tournament and made it to the final round. When we made it to the final, we drew opening government, the first team to present in a British Parliamentary debate, on the motion "This House Would Disband the International Criminal Court." John and I walked out, and he looked at me and asked: "What's the

International Criminal Court?" I said, "I know it is also called the ICC, it is in The Hague, and the U.S. does not like it." My experienced debate partner came up with a great, generic case on the viability of international institutions lacking U.S. participation. You could not tell he did not know what the debate was about. However, our opponent, another friend Dr. Rob Ruiz, had a brief on the ICC and he knew the real facts and that our case was wrong. After Rob finished, it was my turn to speak. I literally stood there babbling incoherently for seven minutes and felt completely embarrassed.

That night I began writing a debate binder that would grow to more than 400 pages, every word written by me and imprinted on my mind. Before this experience, I hated reading; however, the realization of how reading could pay off in immediate tangible award by way of a trophy and intangible award by way of pride, I was hooked. Gaining knowledge only reinforces one's ability to succeed, and confidence enables one to succeed before an audience.

Confidence. The ability to express yourself is an incredibly powerful tool. I have been in plenty of fights, but never have I ended with such a satisfaction than when cutting someone down rhetorically in an argument. While that might not be the most positive aspect of becoming a rhetorician, being able to articulate your desires and convince people to support your ideas is one the best feelings in the world. Once you have passed the bar, opened your own firm, led other organizations, you begin to realize your true potential. Debate not only taught me the importance of taking risks, but gave me the skills and confidence to take a leap of faith.

One evening I was given the opportunity to debate at a retreat for the Board of Trustees for the University of La Verne. Everyone from deans to trustees were in attendance, including the dean of the law school. My debate coach at the time, Ian Lising, introduced me to the audience and my aspirations of attending law school.

After the debate, I was approached by various individuals and ushered to the law school dean. He told me to email him my application and that he would take care of me. The next week I was headed to law school. After that, it was "fake it until I make it" for me. This means that I pretended to belong where I was, no matter where I was and who I was with, and what my true circumstance was.

Competence. Debate is knowing you can do it whether or not you have the right arguments and facts. When you do not have the right answers, it means persuading others that you do. The confidence and abilities debate gives participants sets them apart from other individuals in society. Public speaking is the greatest fear among Americans; being able to simultaneously speak publicly and think critically puts debaters at a distinct advantage. What I have learned leading various organizations is the level of competence needed to be successful is often established at the level of competition. In court, my chances of success are based on my ability to outperform opposing counsel. In a negotiation, my chances of success are based on my ability to secure a better deal than the person on the other side of the negotiation. In board meetings, my ability to successfully pass policies in the organization is often predicated on my ability to outdo the individual arguing against my policy or for a competing alternative.

Speaking Up

This boy born in poverty to a single mother, after living a life of silence, found his voice. Once I learned I had the ability to succeed, not despite my background, but because of it, the sky has been my limit. I went on to open my own law firm immediately after passing the bar. I continue to practice law in my law firm, which has grown several times over and I now practice in five jurisdictions: California, Nevada, New York, Washington State, and Washington, D.C.

I am the President and Founder of a 501(c) (3) nonprofit organization called Social Justice Advocacy Project, Inc. whose mission is to provide empowerment tools to disenfranchised individuals. I serve on the board of directors for five other organizations, including East Valley Community Health Center and the American Mock Trial Association. I coach debate, mock trial, and moot court at the undergraduate and law school level and will likely have completed my second doctoral degree by the time you read this. I have accomplished all of this and so much more, much of which I credit to my participation in debate.

Now is the time for me to end my silence and speak. My answer to "Why debate?" is simple: it gives you the freedom to break your silence and speak your purpose. It will change the trajectory of your life. It will give you an opportunity to participate in and achieve things previously unimaginable. Now, I use the lessons of my life story and the skills I honed in debate, to try to make positive changes in the world. As an attorney, I have fought for people's liberty, including defending a teen against charges of attempted murder that could have led to her spending the rest of her natural life in prison. I have fought for parents to have access to their children, including prosecuting and convicting a father on ninety-five counts of violating a court order for refusing to allow my client access to her children for months. I have sued a number of banks, companies, and individuals who refused to respect the rights of others, and I have filed a number of appeals in cases where I did not feel my clients got the rulings and orders they were entitled to. The audacity with which I have approached my legal career can only be attributed to my participation in debate.

As the Founder and President of my nonprofit, I have actively fought the problems I faced as a child growing up. My organization provides debate courses to the community in domestic violence and homeless shelters. We provide legal clinics to domestic violence victims and individuals with convictions that prevent them from voting. We go above and beyond in our mentoring programs to ensure children do not grow up without the mentorship of a father, even if that mentor is not their biological father.

I am living my dream of service and advocacy only because I learned to research problems, think of and argue solutions, and have the confidence to step out and put those solutions in action. When America was inflamed with anger from the killing of unarmed black individuals by police, I sat down on behalf of my organization with police officers and city council members to propose a platform for reform that I thought was pivotal to the proper way forward. This platform received unimaginable support. The skills you gain as a debater are real.

In the community, I served as President of the West Covina Rotary Club where we had one of the most active years in recent history. I served as Chairman of the board of directors for East Valley Community Health Center and saw the organization through losses of our Chief Financial Officer, Chief Medical Officer, and Chief Operations Officer, while opening one of our largest service locations. I represented both organizations at a round table of community leaders to build the community. I did this at the age of 29 around a table of people two and three times my age. They trusted my leadership and I came through for them. I have coached dozens of people in public speaking competitions like debate and have watched the transformation occur. Debate rounds are artificial, but the advocacy skills and the voice it gives you are very real. This is why I debate.

Thomas Allison was born and raised in Los Angeles, but spent the final years of elementary school to high school in Victorville, California, graduating as a Jackrabbit from Victor Valley High School. Thomas expanded his network outside of the High Desert and wishes to bring lessons and resources that he has witnessed in multiple communities to the High Desert and other places with social needs. Pursuing his fourth degree in law, business, and public administration, Thomas has gained an education that he wants to devote to the people of hurt communities. After successfully starting and growing his law firm, Thomas has acquired meaningful education, experience, and knowledge for the public good. However, it is Thomas' experience in the community that provides him the most knowledge. During his teenage years, Thomas served as a licensed deacon in his church, solidifying a strong moral basis that, despite the inevitable blemish, has remained steadfast. Thomas led several student organizations and headed several philanthropic events. In law school and as a lawyer, he serves on the boards of several community service organizations. Thomas has gained significant leadership experience, education, and skills that he wishes to devote to his community.

Afterword: Supporting Debaters

After reading the essays in this book, we hope you take steps to support students in their pursuit of academic debate. Encourage administrators to start or expand a program in their schools. Ensure coaches get the resources they need to effectively prepare and care for their students. Judge at a local tournament. Provide monetary support for debaters. Provide meals for students or judges at a tournament near you. Conduct a clothing drive or supply drive for the local debate team. Donate old laptops to a local program. The ways you can support students are numerous.

To find a debate program near you, call the nearest school to see if it has a debate program. You can also visit the websites of one of these organizations to find programs near you, discover tournaments near you, and donate resources.

High School Organizations

National Speech & Debate Association (NSDA)

The NSDA (formerly the National Forensic League) is the United States' largest national honor society for students who participate in speech, debate, and interpretation of literature. The NSDA also hosts the largest forensic competition in the world. Every June, roughly 5,000 middle and high school students and coaches from around the world gather for the national championship tournament. The NSDA provides resources for competitors and coaches around the country. You can also find member schools near you.
www.speechanddebate.org/

National Association for Urban Debate Leagues (NAUDL)

The NAUDL and the twenty-two affiliated but independent, urban debate leagues (UDL) around the country ensure that students in urban districts have access to opportunities in academic debate. Every April, the organization brings together the top competitors from each city to compete in the national urban debate championship. From the NAUDL website, you can find contact information for an UDL in your area. Two contributors to this work are staff members for local urban debate leagues. Shawn Briscoe is the Program Director for the St. Louis Urban Debate League (www.stlouisurbandebate.org/), and Amy Cram Helwich is the Executive Director for the Minnesota Urban Debate League (www.augsburg.edu/urbandebateleague/)
http://urbandebate.org/

National Catholic Forensic League (NCFL)

The NCFL provides a network for public and private schools participating in competitive forensics. The organization hosts its own Grand National Tournament every May, bringing together students from across the country. The NCFL website also maintains a list of local leagues and contact information for their directors. The local director can help you find a school with a program near you.
http://ncfl.org/

Undergraduate and Graduate School Organizations

Cross Examination Debate Association (CEDA)

CEDA is a professional association for scholars and teachers in the field of applied argumentation and debate. It is the primary national association promoting policy topic intercollegiate academic debate. It acts as a tournament sanctioning agent, hosts an annual National Championship Tournament, and—in cooperation with the National Debate Tournament (NDT) Committee and the American Debate Association—formulates the annual intercollegiate policy debate topic used by CEDA, NDT, and invitational tournaments throughout the United States. A current list of member schools can be found on its website. www.cedadebate.org/

International Debate Education Association (IDEA)

IDEA is a global network of organizations that value debate as a way to give young people a voice. It works with schools and universities, debate organizations and community groups and partners with foundations, NGOs, businesses, and governments to promote debate, provide training, and make resources available to debaters and coaches around the world. http://idebate.org

World Universities Debating Championships (WUDC)

The WUDC is the world's most prestigious intercollegiate debating championship and adheres to the rules of British Parliamentary Debate. The WUDC is governed by the World Universities Debating Council, a representative body in which each nation attending *Worlds* is able to participate. The Council is led by an Executive Committee. WUDC's website maintains a current institutional ranking where you can find a list of the more than 450 institutions of higher learning that have participated at Worlds in recent years. http://wudc.yaledebate.org/wudctemp/

Other Organizations

Bard Prison Initiative

While not primarily a debate organization, the Bard Prison Initiative (BPI) promotes debate as one of its signature activities. The BPI creates the opportunity for incarcerated men and women to earn a Bard College degree while serving their sentences. The academic standards and workload are rigorous. In addition, it runs a competitive, academic debate program through the Bard Debate Union. The Bard Debate Union integrates debate training and education into the BPI. http://bpi.bard.edu/

Leaders of a Beautiful Struggle (LBS)

LBS is a grassroots political think tank which advances the public policy interest of Black people through youth leadership development, political advocacy, and autonomous intellectual innovation. Although it is not a debate organization, its founders have a background in policy debate, and it supports students who participate in academic debate as a means of societal change.
http://lbsbaltimore.com/

Social Justice Advocacy Project, Inc.

The Social Justice Advocacy Project is a nonprofit organization with the mission of providing empowerment tools to disenfranchised individuals for better self-determination. While it is not a true debate organization, many of its leaders debated competitively while in school and/or coach academic speech and debate. The organization uses speech and debate as empowerment tools through its S.T.R.E.A.M. Academy (Support and Teamwork in Rhetoric, Education, Arts, and Mentorship). Specifically, the Spoken Word Speech & Debate program is designed to empower high school students and members of the community with the skills of critical thinking, argumentation, and debate. Thomas Allison, the President and Founder, is a contributor to this book.
www.advocacyproject.org/

Glossary

Presented here is an alphabetical listing of key words or terms used by authors in this book.

1AC. *See First Affirmative Constructive.*

1AR. *See First Affirmative Rebuttal.*

1NC. *See First Negative Constructive.*

ad hominem. A logical fallacy in which one attacks the individual rather than the argument presented.

affirmative. The pro side of the topic in most American formats of debate.

ballot. The form used by judges to declare the winning side of an academic debate. Many ballots also provide space for judges to rate the effectiveness of debaters, offer constructive criticism, and render a reason for decision.

British Parliamentary (debate). *Also BP.* The most prevalent style of debate for colleges and universities around the world. It is the format practiced at the World Universities Debating Championships. The event features four two-person teams, each receiving an ordinal ranking of first, second, third, or fourth at the conclusion of the round. Topics and sides are assigned for the debaters fifteen minutes prior to the start of the debate.

cards. Quoted evidence used by debaters. The word is a holdover from the days when debaters physically cut quotations and glued them to index cards.

case. Generally refers to the story told by the affirmative team during its initial speech. It can also refer to the story told by the negative team during its first speech.

closed out. A scenario in which the final two remaining teams in a competition hail from the same institution.

congress. *Also congressional debate, student congress.* An American debate format usually limited to high school competitions. Students are assigned to chambers (consisting of ten to thirty members), debate multiple bills or resolutions over the course of several hours, follow parliamentary procedure, and are individually ranked against all other members of the chamber.

counterplan. *Also CP.* A course of action advocated by the negative team as an alternative to the affirmative plan or proposal. It is one of the major offensive arguments used by negative teams in policy debate.

criterion. *Also criteria, value-criterion.* A measure used to determine (or description of) whether a debater's burdens have been met. It is most commonly associated with Lincoln-Douglas debate where a competitor presents a value or principle that should be upheld and a criterion for determining whether that value has been upheld.

cutting cards. The act of turning a published article into usable quotations for a debate. The phrase is a holdover from the days when debaters physically cut quotations and glued them to index cards.

disadvantage. *Also DA, disad.* An unintended consequence of an action. It demonstrates that something bad will happen if a plan is passed. It is one of the main offensive arguments used by negative teams in policy debate.

double turn. Occurs when a debater makes two (strategically) contradictory responses on the same argument; thus, providing a benefit for the opposing team.

drop (an argument). *Also dropped (argument).* Failure to respond to an opponent's argument.

first affirmative constructive. *Also 1AC.* The first speech in a policy debate round.

first affirmative rebuttal. *Also 1AR.* The second speech by the first affirmative speaker in a policy debate round. Sequentially, it is the sixth speech in the debate, following the negative block.

first negative constructive. *Also 1NC.* The first speech by the negative team in a policy debate round. Sequentially, it is the second speech in the debate.

flow. *Also flowing, flows.* The notes of what transpired in a debate round or the act of taking those notes. It usually refers to a very specific method of taking notes that allows participants to track the arguments in a debate as they progress throughout the round. The term derives from the linear way of thinking about arguments found in most American debate formats.

forensic. *Also forensics.* The study of rhetoric or argumentative discourse. It is often used as a term to encompass the academic and competitive discipline of speech, debate, and interpretation of literature.

frame. *Also framing.* The act of shaping how the judge or audience views, weighs, or perceives different issues.

framework. Refers to how judges should evaluate the debate round. What types of arguments matter and what types do not matter? What roles ought debaters play? *See also* **theory.**

impact. Refers to the quantitative and/or qualitative damage of an action or inaction. It is often used, generally, to explain why an argument matters in the debate.

judge. In an academic, competitive debate this is the person assigned to determine the winning and losing debater/teams.

kritik. *Also K.* An argument that challenges the assumptions, logic, or thought processes present in the debate round. It is one of the main offensive arguments used by negative teams in policy debate and is gaining popularity in Lincoln-Douglas debate.

Lincoln-Douglas (debate). *Also LD.* An American format of debate, primarily practiced by high school students. It is a one-on-one format of debate, meaning that one student is assigned to argue in favor of the topic and a second student is assigned to argue against the topic. Traditionally, this format focused on exploring the values or principles that guide decision-making in our society.

line-by-line. The point-for-point discussion on an argument. When viewing the flow of a debate round, one can see the various lines of argument that occurred. The line-by-line refers to examining each line of argument in turn.

link. One of the key elements of a disadvantage or kritik. It explains why an argument applies to the opponent's case/opposing team.

motion. The broad topic to be debated in parliamentary debate formats. Example motions include: This house supports the use of corporal punishment. This house would withdraw all military troops from Afghanistan. This house would ban the personal possession of firearms.

mutually exclusive. The notion that two perspectives or policies cannot coexist. Since policies and ideas advocated by debaters are thought of as *competing* policy options, interpretations, or perspectives, the two teams' advocacies ought to be mutually exclusive.

national circuit. High school tournaments in the United States that draw competitors from across the nation or a geographic region. Students who do well at these tournaments are often rewarded with qualifying legs for the Tournament of Champions hosted by the University of Kentucky.

negative. The con side of the topic in most American formats of debate.

negative block. *Also the block.* The point in policy debate and some parliamentary formats where the negative team has back-to-back speeches. Most members of the debate community conceptualize policy debate's second negative constructive and the first negative rebuttal as a single speech given by two debaters.

net benefit. An additional advantage achieved with a competing advocacy. For example, a counterplan or counter model may accrue an additional advantage that the affirmative's plan does not achieve.

paradigm. The lens through which one views debate. Judges hold different views about what debate should look like, what is acceptable and not acceptable, the types of arguments that should be run in debate rounds, and how debates should be evaluated.

parliamentary (debate). *Also parli.* A categorization of debate events primarily found at the college level. A key feature of parliamentary debate is that it is extemporaneous in nature, meaning that topics are usually announced fifteen or twenty minutes before the start of the debate. A second defining feature of parliamentary debate is a prohibition on using quoted evidence during speeches.

permutation. *Also perm.* A test of competition between the affirmative and negative advocacies to determine if the plan and counterplan or the affirmative and the alternative can coexist. An affirmative team may offer a perm to show how its advocacy can be combined with the negative's advocacy.

plan. *Also plan text.* In policy debate, the affirmative team presents a proposal or course of action that serves as the basis of its advocacy throughout the debate round. While the affirmative can craft any proposal it can imagine, the policy is still limited by the boundaries established by the resolution or debate topic.

policy (debate). *Also cross-examination debate, CX debate, team debate.* An American debate format practiced in both high school and college. The format consists of two two-person teams assigned to opposite sides of the resolution. The early speeches in the debate round are (usually) heavily built on lengthy quotations, with most of the analysis, depth of discussion, and framing of issues coming in later speeches. Traditionally, it was defined by a specific policy proposal or plan presented by the affirmative team.

public forum. *Also PF, PUF, PuFo, PFD.* A predominantly American event practiced at the high school level. It consists of two two-person teams. Discussions focus on current events and change monthly.

reason for decision. The judge's explanation for how he or she determined the winner of a debate contest.

resolution. The broad topic to be debated. It is usually set by a governing organization such as the National Speech & Debate Association or the Cross Examination Debate Association.

solvency. A central element of an affirmative case in policy debate. It refers to the affirmative plan's ability to reduce or eliminate the harms found in the status quo. Generally, it refers to a proposal's ability to fix a problem.

speed. The rate at which a debater speaks. Generally, it is used to refer to the tactic of speaking at an incredibly high rate of delivery.

spread. The number of arguments presented against an opponent and/or the number of individual responses to a specific argument. Generally, it is used to refer to the tactic of placing a large number of arguments and/or responses on the flow.

status quo. *Also SQ, squo.* The present system. The way things are now.

stock issues. The central elements required to build a compelling case. It is most often associated with policy debate. In policy, an affirmative case contains five core elements (or stock issues): significance, harms, inherency, topicality, and solvency.

student congress. *See congress.*

tagline. *Also tag.* A one-sentence summary of a piece of evidence or analytical response.

theory. *Also theory debate.* The portion of the debate in which students discuss how the game (of debate) should be played, how the judge should evaluate the round, and so on.

topicality. *Also T.* One of the five stock issues of an affirmative case in policy debate. Affirmative plans must fall within the parameters established by the resolution.

tub(s). A storage container, such as a Rubbermaid tub, used to carry debaters' cases, additional research (files), and supplies. Essentially, tubs are portable filing cabinets. With the advent of low-cost laptops and tablets, fewer debaters are relying on paper copies of their files in competition and tubs are becoming less common at debate tournaments.

turn. *Also case turn, impact turn, link turn.* The act of taking an argument run by your opponents and turning it against them.

uniqueness. One of the key elements of a disadvantage. It explains that the disadvantage is not going to occur in the status quo, but will occur if the affirmative plan is passed.

voters. The impacts of any procedural or rule of the game argument. They are the explanation for why an argument will win a debate round. Usually, voters reference the rules of the game, fair competition, or educational benefit.

voting issue(s). The elements considered by judges to determine the outcome of a competition. The things they evaluate when ascertaining a student's contributions, effectiveness, and so forth.

About the Lead Author and Editor

Shawn F. Briscoe began his journey in academic debate more than 25 years ago. He is an ardent believer in the educational merits of interscholastic forensics. To that effect, he has authored various articles for *Principal Leadership*, *Education Next*, and *Rostrum*. He also wrote the textbook, *Policy Debate: A Guide for High School & College Debaters*, for Southern Illinois University Press. He believes the activity promotes authentic learning of concepts at the heart of the standard curriculum, while doing so in a unique environment that is competitive, cooperative, social, and extremely fun!

Shawn has coached and taught at both the high school and the collegiate levels; in multiple debate, speech, and interpretation of literature events; at schools across the country; and on local, regional, national, and international circuits. His philosophy is that the activity should primarily be about promoting growth and education, while secondarily being a fun activity for the participants has proven competitively successful.

Shawn currently serves as the Program Director for the St. Louis Urban Debate League.

Visit his website for additional resources: mydebateresource.com

Made in the USA
Middletown, DE
22 March 2020